D1478249

Group Technology

International Series in
Management Science/Operations Research

Series Editor:
James P. Ignizio
   The Pennsylvania State University, U.S.A.

Advisory Editors:

Thomas Saaty
   University of Pittsburgh, U.S.A.
Katsundo Hitomi
   Kyoto University, Japan
H.-J. Zimmermann
   RWTH Aachen, West Germany
B.H.P. Rivett
   University of Sussex, England

Group Technology

Applications to Production Management

Inyong Ham
The Pennsylvania State University

Katsundo Hitomi
Kyoto University

Teruhiko Yoshida
Kobe University of Commerce

Kluwer-Nijhoff Publishing
a member of the Kluwer Academic Publishers Group

Boston-Dordrecht-Lancaster

Distributors for North America:
Kluwer Academic Publishers
190 Old Derby Street
Hingham, MA 02043, U.S.A.

Distributors Outside North America:
Kluwer Academic Publishers Group
Distribution Centre
P.O. Box 322
3300AH Dordrecht, The Netherlands

Library of Congress Cataloging in Publication Data

Ham, Inyong, 1925–
  Group technology.

  (International series in management science/operations
research)
  Includes index.
  1. Production management. 2. Group technology.
I. Hitomi, Katsundo, 1932–   . II. Yoshida, Teruhiko,
1946–   . III. Title. IV. Series.
TS155.H2812 1984   658.5'1   84-5742
ISBN 0-89838-090-1

Printed in the United States of America

Contents

Preface

Mass production and mass consumption, so far considered virtues in a free economic soceity, have changed. Various problems have occurred including economic stagnation, energy crisis, shortage of material resources, proliferation of pollution, lack of skilled labor, rapid changes of product design, technical innovation, and others. Moreover, individual manufacturing firms must take steps to adopt multi-product, small-lot-sized (batch type) production as a type of production in order to adapt themselves to a market movement characterized by a diversified and specialty-oriented society and a short product life cycle. The number of manufacturing firms worldwide that use a type of multi-product, small-lot-sized production is expected to increase. This is so even in the United States, which has been said to be a country of mass production.

Multi-product, small-lot-sized production has been considered to be a milestone to flow-type mass production, which has been thought to be the most effective production system. Intensive efforts have been made to investigate mass production systems from both theoretical and practical viewpoints. Few studies have been made for multi-product, small-lot-sized production (batch-type manufacturing). Considering the present business circumstances faced with various difficulties, it is strongly required to establish some theories useful for making practically effective and flexible multi-product, small-lot-sized production systems.

Several effective approaches to the batch-type manufacturing systems have been developed. Group technology (GT) is one such method that has steadily obtained great interest from progressive manufacturing firms all over the world. This is a manufacturing philosophy or concept to increase production efficiency by identifying and exploiting the sameness or similarity of parts and operation processes in design and manufacturing. By applying group technology, several advantages, including mass production effect, the possibility of a flow-shop pattern on the process route, reduction of setup time and cost, simplification of material flow and handling, rationalization of design, standardization of production processes, are expected.

So far, intensive efforts have been made to apply group technology concepts for higher manufacturing productivity by various countries, institutes, and industries around the world. Our laboratories, Manufacturing Systems Laboratory at the Department of Industrial and Management Systems Engineering (I. Ham), The Pennsylvania State University in the United States, and Production Management Systems Laboratory (headed by K. Hitomi) at the School of Mechanical Engineering, Kyoto University, in Japan, have done some research in collaboration on the applications of group technology to production management from the standpoints of production engineering, management science, and systems engineering. Based on the results of this cooperative research, this book is intended to describe a group technology approach to multi-product, small-lot-sized production management.

This book consists of ten chapters, with each chapter presenting the following contents:

Chapter 1 describes the basic characteristics of and effective approaches to multi-product, small-lot-sized (or jobbing) production and the important role of group technology for this type of production.

Chapter 2 describes the principles of group technology, including its history, basic classification and coding systems, and advice for how to apply group technology to production management.

Chapter 3 treats process planning for group technology applications. Essentials of process planning, which is a microscopic decision for determining the optimum production process routes, are explained. Basic models of process planning are mentioned and extended process planning models to which group technology is applied are introduced for selecting optimal process routes for converting raw materials into finished parts or products from among several alternative process routes by considering the commonality of a tooling method and by utilizing reduction of setup time.

Chapter 4 deals with production planning for group technology applications. Essentials of production planning, which is a function of determining kinds of product items and quantities to be produced in specified time periods, are explained. Product-mix planning models and production lot-sizing models for determining lot size in intermittent production are analyzed on the basis of the concept of group technology.

Chapter 5 treats machine loading for group technology applications. Essentials of machine loading are explained, and basic models are introduced. Machine loading models for group technology applications, which are referred to as group machine loading models, are constructed on the assumption that jobs (parts) to be processed are classified into several groups based on the concept of group technology. Optimal algorithms are proposed to determine the combination of kinds of groups and jobs to be processed on single-stage and multi-stage production systems.

Chapter 6 considers group machine loading models with variable processing times, in which processing times required to complete specified operations of jobs are variable depending on machining conditions. Usually processing times and costs for producing parts are considered constant. In reality, however, they vary significantly depending on production conditions, such as machining speeds, spindle speeds of machine tools, feed rates, and so on. In this chapter, optimal machining speeds as well as optimal kinds of groups and jobs to be processed are theoretically determined.

Chapter 7 deals with production scheduling for group technology applications. Essentials of production scheduling are stated, and basic models are explained. These basic models are extended to production scheduling models for group technology applications, which are referred to as group production scheduling models. In group production scheduling, both of the sequence of groups classified and the sequence of jobs are to be determined. Single-stage group production scheduling models are analyzed in the last section of this chapter.

Chapter 8 deals with multi-stage group production scheduling. Algorithms for optimally or near-optimally determining the sequences of groups and jobs are proposed based on three typical approaches to production scheduling—: theoretical, branch-and-bound, and heuristic approaches. Group production scheduling with variable processing times is also discussed in this chapter.

Chapter 9 treats layout planning for group technology applications. Essentials of layout planning, a function of determining a spatial location for a collection of production facilities in a production plant, are stated, and basic models of layout planning are explained. Layout planning models for group technology applications are constructed to optimally determine group technology layouts. Decision procedures are developed to determine machine-part grouping (GT cell).

Chapter 10 includes integration of group technology and other related topics, such as GT and MRP, GT and CAD/CAM, and GT and engineering economy.

The authors are pleased to publish this book as one of the International Series in Management Science/Operations Research of Kluwer-Nijhoff Publishing.

The authors are deeply indebted to Dr. James P. Ignizio, Chief Editor of this series and Professor of Industrial Engineering at The Pennsylvania State University, to Mr. Philip D. Jones, former Director, and to Ms. Bernadine Richey, Managing Editor, Kluwer-Nijhoff Publishing, for their decision to publish and assistance in publishing this book.

Spring 1984

Inyong Ham
Katsundo Hitomi
Teruhiko Yoshida

Group Technology

1 INTRODUCTION

1.1 Multi-Product, Small-Lot-Sized Production

The 1980s are said to be an era of low economic growth, resource saving, and energy saving. Mass production and mass consumption, which had been considered to be a virtue in the 1960s and 1970s, have been changed. Moreover, the consumer's sense of value has gained variety through the age of the affluent. Thus individuals' desires to possess special goods have risen and the life cycle of products has decreased. These situations gradually have caused many firms to manufacture products in a specified, short time period, and the production volume for each product is very low. This type of production is called "multi-product, small-lot-sized production," "batch-type production," or "variety production," and is mainly production-to-order. In multi-product, small-lot-sized production, the material flow for producing each of the products is dissimilar and complicated, unlike mass production. Characteristics of multi-product, small-lot-sized production are [1]:

1. variety of product items
2. variety of production processes
3. complexity of productive capacity
4. uncertainty of outside conditions

1

5. difficulty of production planning and scheduling
6. dynamic situation of implementation and control of production

1.2 Effective Approaches to Multi-Product, Small-Lot-Sized Production

To cope with difficulties in multi-product, small-lot-sized production, several approaches have been developed as follows [1]:

1. **Industrial engineering.** Industrial engineering (IE) is a traditional methodology of production organization and management mainly based upon the pioneering works in the field of scientific management by F.W. Taylor. The Institute of Industrial Engineers defines *industrial engineering* as concern with the design, improvement, and installation of integral systems of people, materials, machines, energy, and information. It draws on specialized knowledge and skill in the mathematical, physical, and social sciences, together with the principles and methods of engineering analysis and design, to specify, predict, and evaluate the results to be obtained from such systems.

The basic principles of IE are standardization, simplification, and specialization. Above all, standardization plays a critical role in rationalizing multi-product, small-lot-sized production as follows:

a) Standardization of products; setting standard products, thus reducing kinds of product items.
b) Standardization of parts; setting standard parts and producing products mainly by combining such parts.
c) Standardization of materials; employing standard raw materials as much as possible.
d) Standardization of process routes; establishing standard process routes, through which parts are manufactured and products are assembled.

2. **Group Technology.** Group technology (GT) is a concept to increase production efficiency by grouping various parts and products with similar design and/or production process. The application of GT results in the mass production effect to multi-product, small-lot-sized production. This technique is the main subject of this book and is detailed in the subsequent chapters.

3. **Part-oriented production system.** Although a variety of products differ from each other in terms of outward appearance, the same components

are often contained in them. Such components are produced according to the results of demand or sales forecasts for stock in advance to receiving orders and are positively stocked as parts inventory in the parts center. A variety of products are assembled on the receipt of orders by suitably combining parts from the parts center. With this way of production, production lead time from the order received to the finished product is decreased to only the time required for assembly. This type of production is called a "part-oriented production."

In the activities of manufacturing firms, in addition to the production function, the marketing or sales function plays an important role. A part-oriented production system can be regarded as an order-entry system from the marketing viewpoint. In this system, the customer can decide the parts content and structure of the product at the time of ordering. The manufacturer then inquires into products and parts in store, which are required to satisfy a customer's order. Parts explosion, materials planning, manufacturing order for deficient parts, assembly scheduling, due-date control, inquiry into the progress of production, and other managerial and operational works are carried out accurately and at the right time by a central computer connected with remote terminals in each business office on an on-line, real-time basis. This system is employed by automobile manufacturers and home-appliance makers.

4. **On-line production management.** An effective approach to multi-product, small-lot-sized production is to control individual operations in the dynamic job shop by installing terminals at work centers, which communicate with a control computer in an on-line mode. Thus, as they are generated, various production data are collected at the work centers and transmitted into the control department, where rapid data processing by computer makes it possible to construct a new schedule relating to future production activities. This is then transmitted back to the work centers. This type of system is called an "on-line production management system." By employing this system, effective management is possible for multi-product, small-lot-sized production.

5. **Flexible manufacturing.** The wide variety of product demand tends to promote considerable uncertainty as to factors of production such as production facilities, human labor, and raw materials. Therefore, in order to overcome difficulties involved in multi-product, small-lot-sized production, the highest degree of flexibility in these factors is required. The production that has flexibility in factors of production will be called "flexible manufacturing."

Among factors of production, the flexibility of production facilities is strongly required since production facilities usually need a high capital investment. Representative of facilities having high flexibility is a numerically controlled (NC) machine tool.

A numerically controlled manufacturing system with computer, the DNC (direct numerical control) system, which is the most advanced automated production system, has an ability to meet variety production rather than mass production. In the flexible-type DNC system, a number of numerically controlled machines including machining centers, robots, and an automated conveyor system are connected together to a control computer for producing a number of parts having various shapes and process routes. The parts to be processed in this system are, according to instructions from the control computer, sequentially transferred to their appropriate machine tools and finished. This automated system is one method of variety production and is often called a "flexible manufacturing system" (FMS).

6. **Material requirements planning or manufacturing resource planning (MRP).** This is a kind of production planning and control system which is effective for discrete-part production such as automobile production. Based on a master production schedule of end-product items, MRP principally calculates the requirements of components of different levels of bill of materials and determines the exact times of need for those components by making use of information on an item master data file and an inventory file. The basic procedure of MRP consists of computations of gross requirements and net requirements for different levels of components, lot sizing (determination of planned order coverage), and releasing the planned orders. Morever, MRP includes machine loading and even shop floor control.

1.3 Group Technology Applications to Production Management

Several books on group technology have already been published [2–8]. However, main topics that these books have covered are mostly technological aspects of group technology applications; classification and coding systems, design rationalization, jig and fixture design for group processing, group technology layout (or GT cell formation), et cetera. In order to achieve additional benefits from group technology, the philosophy of group technology should be applied to other production management areas [9]. The purpose of this book is to cover applications of group technology to several fields of production management, such as process planning, production planning, production scheduling, layout planning, and others.

References

1. Hitomi, K. *Manufacturing Systems Engineering*. London: Taylor & Francis, Ltd., 1979, pp. 30–34.
2. Mitrofanov, S.P. *Scientific Principles of Group Technology* (Russian text published in 1959). Translated into English by E. Harris, National Lending Library for Science and Technology, U.K., 1966.
3. Edwards, G.A.B. *Readings in Group Technology*. London: The Machinery Publishing Co., 1971.
4. Gallagher, C.C., and Night, W.A. *Group Technology*. London: Butterworth & Co., 1973.
5. Burbidge, J.L. *The Introduction of Group Technology*. London: John Wiley & Sons, Inc., 1975.
6. Arn, E.A. *Group Technology*. New York: Springer-Verlag, 1975.
7. Burbidge, J.L. *Group Technology in the Engineering Industry*. London: Mechanical Engineering Publications, 1979.
8. Hyde, W.F. *Improving Productivity by Classification, Coding, and Data Base Standardization*. New York: Marcel Dekker, 1981.
9. Hitomi, K. (ed.) *Production Management Systems by Group Technology* (Japanese), Tokyo: Daily Technical Newspaper Co., 1981.

2 BASIC PRINCIPLES OF GROUP TECHNOLOGY

2.1 Introduction

Group technology (GT) is a manufacturing philosophy that identifies and exploits the underlying sameness of parts and manufacturing processes. In batch-type manufacturing for multi-products and small-lot-sized production, conventionally each part is treated as unique from design through manufacture [1,2,3,4,5]. However, by grouping similar parts into part families based on either their design or processes, it is possible to increase the productivity through more effective design rationalization and data retrieval, and manufacturing standardization and rationalization. The basic concept of group technology has been practiced around the world for many years as part of "good engineering practice" and "scientific management" [6]. Applications of group technology concepts are usually identified under different names and in various forms of engineering and manufacturing functions. Traditionally, group technology practices were limited to conventional batch-type manufacturing for productivity improvement, with different degrees of success either in the design or manufacturing areas. For many years, group technology did not receive the formal recognition it deserves and has not been rigorously practiced as a systematic approach to productivity improvements. Recently, however, development and implementation of

7

computer-integrated manufacturing (CIM) led to a renewed interest in group technology since it provides the essential means for higher manufacturing productivity for successful integration of CAD/CAM through the application of the part-family concept [7].

World trends in advanced manufacturing are dynamic and evolutionary. It is true that the advancement of industrial technology has been very significant in recent decades, but we are still in the early stages of a technical revolution in manufacturing, especially in the area of integrated computer applications in manufacturing. Although the world is composed of very complex societies supported by many activities, manufacturing is still the prime wealth-producing activity of not only industrialized but also some developing nations today [8]. Naturally, many countries are well aware of this fact and have major national efforts underway to improve manufacturing technology and productivity.

One of the most important current problems in increasing manufacturing productivity is the economic incentive. Manufacturing normally contributes a major portion of the gross national product to industrialized countries. Yet in spite of this, manufacturing is not the highly productive and efficient activity that many believe it to be.

For example, this is clearly true of a batch-type manufacturing environment. It has been reported that in batch-type metalworking shops, only about 5 percent of the total production time is actually spent on machine tools while the remaining 95 percent of the time is spent in moving and waiting for parts in the shop. Of that 5 percent, only about 30 percent is spent as productive time in cutting materials as shown in figure 2.1 [9]. Therefore, major efforts

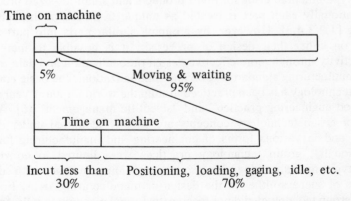

Figure 2.1. Percentage of the life of the average workpiece in batch-type metal cutting production shop [9]

should be made to improve this situation for higher manufacturing productivity. Another area for improvement is more efficient utilization of expensive machine tools and facilities along with increased productivity from the labor force.

In recent years—because of the rapidly growing sophistication of world manufacturing technology that is largely due to the advent of the computer and its many and varied applications—major attention and effort in advanced manufacturing technology has been directed to the control, automation, and optimization of manufacturing. It should also be noted that strong new economic and social pressures have been influencing the manufacturing industry a great deal in areas such as manufacturing productivity, manufacturing costs, job satisfaction or enrichment, environmental controls, et cetera. In modern manufacturing industry, one of the significant facts to be carefully examined is the change in production trends. A recent survey of group technology applications in the metalworking industry in the United States shows that the average lot size is less than 50 pieces [10]. The current trend indicates that the percentage of batch-type manufacturing has been increasing. Thus the potential for economic improvement of manufacturing by group technology is indeed not only tremendous now but will grow in time.

2.2 Part Family Formation and GT Cell

A part family is a group of parts that have some specific sameness and similarities in design features or production processes. Examples of two basic types of part families are shown in figure 2.2. A part family may be grouped with the parts having similar design features such as geometric shape, size, materials, et cetera, while a part family may be grouped with respect to production operations, that is, machines, processes, operations, tooling, et cetera.

In grouping part families, it is important to consider the production data such as lot size, frequency, time, annual production plan, et cetera in scheduling for optimum sequencing and machine loading. Part family grouping is an important step for successful group technology applications. Four basic methods are used to form part families:

1. manual/visual search
2. nomenclatures/functions
3. production flow analysis
4. classification and coding systems

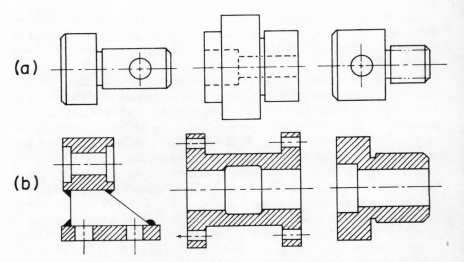

Figure 2.2. Examples of part families. (a) Similar in shape and geometry and (b) similar in production operation processes.

The manual search is simple but very much limited in its scope to deal with a large number of parts. It has been proven that nomenclatures and functions are not reliable for effective grouping. Therefore, it has been a common practice to use either production flow analysis or classification and coding method in forming part families and machine groups or cells for group technology applications.

Production flow analysis is a method for forming part families and/or machine groups/cells by analyzing the production process data listed in operation sheets, that is, machine/workstations, operations, operation sequences, et cetera [11,12]. This method does not require a classification and coding system, but it needs reliable, well-documented operation sheets.

A classification and coding system provides an effective means for forming part families based on the specific parameters and code digits of the system regardless of the origin or use of the part [2,13,14,15,16]. Also it should be noted that a well-designed and properly adapted classification and coding system provides an effective data retrieval system for common data base, which is essential for successful implementation of CIM.

2.3 Classification and Coding System

Group technology may be practiced without a classification and coding system. Yet it is an essential and effective tool for successful implementation of group technology concept, in particular for implementation of CIM. The term *classification* means to sort parts into groups thus separating parts with similarities and/or dissimilarities based on some predetermined parameters. A *code* may be numbers or letters or a combination of numbers and/or letters which are assigned to the parts for information processing.

Many different types of classification and coding systems have been developed and used around the world. Selected examples of worldwide classification and coding systems are shown in table 2.1. An example of a coded part using a publicly available system is shown in figure 2.3 [17].

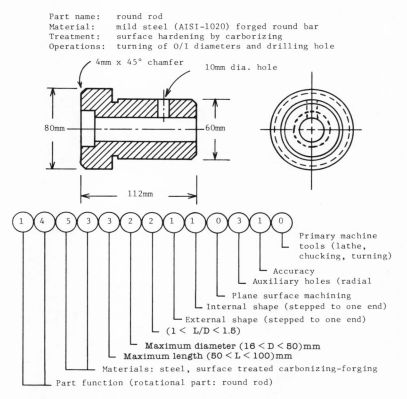

Figure 2.3. Coded example using a classification and coding system (refer to figure 2.4(b))

Table 2.1. Selected Examples of Worldwide Classification and Coding Systems

SYSTEM	ORGANIZATION AND COUNTRY
OPITZ	Aachen Tech. Univ. (W. Germany)
OPITZ's SHEET METAL	Aachen Tech. Univ. (W. Germany)
STUTTGART	Univ. of Stuttgart (W. Germany)
PITTLER	Pittler Mach. Tool Co. (W. Germany)
GILDEMEISTER	Gildemeister Co. (W. Germany)
ZAFO	(W. Germany)
SPIES	(W. Germany)
PUSCHMAN	(W. Germany)
DDR	DDR Standard (E. Germany)
WALTER	(E. Germany)
AUERSWALD	(E. Germany)
MITROFANOV	(USSR)
LITMO	Leningrad Inst. for Pre & Optics (USSR)
NIITMASH	(USSR)
VPTI	(USSR)
GUREVICH	(USSR)
VUOSO	Prague M/T Res. Inst. (Czechoslovakia)
VUSTE	Res. Inst. Eng. Tech. & Econ. (Czech.)
MALEK	(Czechoslovakia)
IAMA	IAMA (Yugoslavia)
PERA	Prod. Engr. Res. Assn. (U.K.)
SALFORD	(U.K.)
PGM	PGM, Ltd. (Sweden)
KC-1	(Japan)
KC-2	(Japan)
KK-1	(Japan)
KK-2	(Japan)
KK-3	(Japan)
SHEET METAL SYSTEM	(Japan)
CASTING SYSTEM	(Japan)
HITACHI	Hitachi Co. (Japan)
TOYODA	Toyoda, Ltd. (Japan)
TOSHIBA	Toshiba Machine Co., Ltd. (Japan)
BRISCH	Brisch-Birn, Inc. (U.K. and U.S.A.)
MICLASS	TNO (Holland and U.S.A.)
CODE	Mfg. Data Systems, Inc. (U.S.A.)
PARTS ANALOG	Lovelace, Lawrence & Co., Inc. (U.S.A.)
ALLIS CHALMERS	Allis Chalmers (U.S.A.)
SAGT	Purdue Univ. (U.S.A.)
BUCCS	Boeing Co., (U.S.A.)
ASSEMBLY PART CODE	Univ. of Massachusetts (U.S.A.)
HOLE CODE	Purdue University (U.S.A.)
DTH/DCLASS	Brigham Young Univ. (U.S.A.)
CINCLASS	Cincinnati Milacron Co. (U.S.A.)

Adaptation and implementation of a classification and coding system for group technology applications is an important and complex task. Although many systems are available, each company should search for or develop a system suited to its needs and requirements. One of the essential requirements of a well-designed classification and coding system for group technology applications is to group part families as needed, based on specified parameters and should be capable of effective data retrieval for various functions as required. An example of part family grouping using a classification and coding system (figure 2.4) is shown in figure 2.5.

Other types of classification and coding systems for general purposes have been developed and are used by many government agencies and service sectors, for such areas as libraries, museums, office supplies, commodities, insurance, credit cards, et cetera. One of the important factors in selecting a classification and coding system is to maintain a balance between the amount of information needed and the number of digit columns required to provide this information.

Even though it is well recognized that a classification and coding system is a key element for full exploitation of the group technology benefits, in fact a classification and coding system as a tool and suitable system is just a prerequisite first step for group technology applications. After installing a suitable system, further efforts should be made to rationalize design works, standardize process plans, optimize production scheduling (group scheduling), group tooling set-ups, improve inventory and purchasing requirements, et cetera, through maximum utilization of a classification and coding system for effective data retrieval.

2.4 Design Rationalization

One of the most important and practical benefits of successful group technology applications, in particular, using a well-designed classification and coding system, is design data retrieval and design rationalization. In having a system and data file of part families and the capability to retrieve design data of desired part families, it is possible to rationalize design process through comparative analysis of the proposed design with the existing designs. Design decisions can be made: a) use as it is when an old design is available; b) modify and use it if there is a similar design; and c) design a new part when no part family exists [18]. Design rationalization efforts using group technology concept provide the following features:

1. effective part family grouping
2. effective design information/data retrieval

COLUMN	I	II	III	IV	V	VI	VII	VIII	IX	X	XI	XII	XIII
	PARTS NAME (FUNCTION)		MATERIALS		MAIN DIMENSIONS		PRIMAL SHAPES, RATIO OF MAIN DIMENSIONS	GEOMETRICAL SHAPES AND MACHINING				ACCURACY	MAIN MACHINING TOOLS AT PRIMAY STAGE
	GENERAL CLASSIFICATION	DETAIL CLASSIFICATION	GENERAL CLASSIFICATION	DETAIL CLASSIFICATION	(R) L / (N) A	(R) D / (N) B		(R) EXTERNAL SHAPE / (N) PLANE SURFACE	(R) INTERNAL SHAPE / (N) PRINCIPAL BORES	(R) PLANE SURFACE MACHINING / (N) SPECIAL MACHINING	(R) AUXILIARY HOLES / (N) DITTO		
	MATRIX	DITTO	MATRIX	DITTO	SEPARATE TABLES FOR ROTATIONAL (R) AND NON-ROTATIONAL (N) COMPONENTS	DITTO	DITTO	DITTO	DITTO	DITTO	DITTO	COMMON TABLE FOR R AND N	DITTO
POSITIONS													
0													
1													
2													
3													
4													
5													
6													
7													
8													
9													

Figure 2.4. Basic code structure of a publicly available classification and coding system (Japanese KK-1 system) [17]

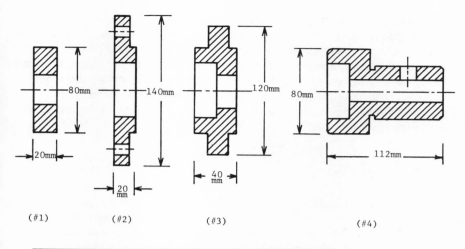

Part No.	Code Number												
#1	4	0	1	1	1	2	0	0	1	0	0	1	0
#2	4	1	1	1	1	3	0	1	1	0	2	1	0
#3	4	1	1	1	1	3	0	4	1	0	0	1	0
#4	1	4	5	3	3	2	2	1	1	0	3	1	0

(Japanese KK-1 Classification & Coding System)

Figure 2.5. Examples of classification and coding and part-family grouping

3. standardization and simplification
4. optimum design for economic manufacture
5. elimination/reduction of duplicate designs
6. common data base for integrated CAD/CAM

2.5 Group Production

2.5.1 Machine Group/Cell

For production applications of group technology concept, a group of machines for a part family or more may be formed to process the parts that have similar or the same operations using the machines. Since the machines are laid out as a group/cell, the parts flow in a semi-flow line minimizing transportation and waiting, thus reducing throughput time. Examples of group technology layout of machines are exhibited in figure 9.4.

In recent years, a modern machining center was introduced and operates characteristically the same as a machine group/cell of conventional machine tools. These groups of machining centers are sometimes defined as manufacturing cells, multi-station manufacturing systems, or flexible manufacturing systems.

2.5.2 Group Tooling

To process a part family that requires a similar tooling and tooling set-up, it is logical to design a group jig/fixture to accommodate the tooling requirements of the part family. Usually these group jigs/fixtures are designed to accept all members of the family accompanied with adapters that meet the specific needs and differences of the parts in the family. With a group jig/fixture, there is no need to design each individual toolings for each part. Most adapters are very inexpensive compared to the regular jigs/ fixtures. Therefore, obviously this saves a great deal of tooling costs and also set-up costs. Economic analysis of group tooling practice is discussed in chapter 10.

2.5.3 Numerical Control Part Programming

The group technology concept has been adapted for software development of numerical control (NC) machining which is referred to as "part-family programming." Part-family programming is similar to a group tooling method, that is, a NC programming method using a master computer program to accommodate common or similar program elements for a part family. Therefore, part-family programming practice reduces the NC operation costs by reducing such factors as programming time, manpower, and tape proveout time.

2.6 Group Technology Production Management

In order to achieve the higher productivity and efficiency in batch-type manufacturing, it is absolutely essential to incorporate the concept of group technology into every manufacturing activity including operations and management. So far, many efforts have been made to apply the group technology concept to the technological aspects of manufacturing activities such as classification and coding systems, design rationalization, GT cells design for group tooling, and others.

Recently, intensive attention is being given to the CAD/CAM system as the application of computers is expanded, and the important roles of GT applications for CIM have been recognized. From this point of view, production management aspects of group technology applications have gained great interest in such areas as computer-aided process planning and computerized group scheduling.

2.6.1 Computer-Aided Process Planning

One of the key requirements for the successful implementation of CIM is computer-aided process planning [19]. An automated process planning technique is a basis for a rational and logical approach to improve manufacturing productivity in a CIM system. Group technology plays an essential role for programming of computer-automated process planning, based on the part-family concept of group technology (refer to chapter 10; 10.2.2).

2.6.2 Production Control and Scheduling

General production scheduling problems are complex and difficult to optimize. The group technology approach based on part-family grouping for scheduling simplifies the problems regardless of whether part families are processed through a machine group/cell or not [20]. Production scheduling based on the group technology concept is called "group scheduling" [21–25]. Appropriate application of group scheduling effectively reduces total throughput time and results in the reduction of work-in-process inventory.

To solve the group scheduling problems, many algorithms and mathematical models have been developed, and related computer programs were also developed to schedule jobs of a part-family or part families [26]. The specific objectives of these algorithms and models are to optimize such features as operations sequencing and machine loading. This book covers in great detail this subject (see chapters 5, 6, 7, and 8).

It should be understood that group scheduling alone cannot be effective unless it is well coordinated with related production planning and control activities. The integrated applications of group scheduling and Material

Requirements Planning (MRP) is very essential for successful implementation of both activities (refer to chapter 10; 10.1) [27].

2.7 Group Technology and Automated Factory Systems

A current trend for automated factory systems indicates increased usages of DNC, CNC, machining centers, industrial robots, microprocessors, et cetera and moves toward more computer-integrated manufacturing systems. The automated factory systems built currently worldwide are essentially based on an hierarchical computer control system of automated manufacturing cell systems. This means that the basic concept for such a system is based on the use of group technology cells, each devoted to the production of a given family of parts (refer to chapter 10; 10.2.4).

References

1. Mitrofanov, S.P. *Scientific Principles of Group Technology*. (English translation), edited by J. Grayson, London: National Lending Library for Science and Technology, U.K., 1966.
   _____. *Scientific Principles of Group Technology*. (Russian), Moscow, 1970.
   _____. *Scientific Principles of Machine Building Production*. (Russian), Moscow, 1976.
2. Gallagher, C.C., and Knight, W.A. *Group Technology*. London: Butterworths, 1973.
3. Burbidge, J.L. *The Introduction of Group Technology*. New York: John Wiley & Sons, 1975.
4. Edwards, G.A.B. *Readings in Group Technology*. London: Machinery Pub. Co., 1971.
5. Ham, I. Introduction of Group Technology, *SME Technical Paper*, MMR-76-03, February; also CAM-I Seminars Proceedings, June, 1975, (No. P-75-ppp-01) and January 1976 (No. P-76-ppp-01).
6. Hathaway, H.D. "The Mnemonic Systems of Classification; As Used in the Taylor System of Management." *Industrial Management*, 9(3), (September 1920), pp. 173–183.
7. Ham, I. "Current Trends and Future Prospects of Group Technology Applications Related to Integrated Computer Aided Manufacturing." *Proceedings of Conference on International Manufacturing Engineering*, 1980, published by the Institution of Engineers, Australia, August 1980.

8. Merchant, M.E. "Progress and Problems in the Application of New Optimization Technology in Manufacturing." *CIRP Annals*, 1968.
9. Carter, C.F., Jr. "Trends in Machine Tool Development and Applications." Proceedings of 2nd International Conference on Product Development and Manufacturing Technology, 1971, London: MacDonald & Co., 1972.
10. Ham, I., and Reed, W. "Preliminary Survey Results on Group Technology Applications in Metal Working." Technical Paper #MS77-328, Society of Manufacturing Engineers, 1977.
11. Burbidge, J.L. *"Production Planning."* London: Heineman, 1971.
12. Burbidge, J.L. *Proceedings of International Seminar on Group Technology*, International Center for Advanced Technical & Vocational Training, Turin, Italy, 1969.
13. Opitz, H. *"A Classification System to Describe Workpieces* (Parts I & II)." London & New York: 1970. Pergaman Press, 1970.
14. Gombinski, J., "Fundamental Aspect of Component Classification." *CIRP Annals* 17 (1969), pp. 367–375.
15. Hyde, W.F. *"Improving Productivity by Classification Coding and Data Base Standardization."* New York and Basel: Marcel Dekker, Inc., 1981.
16. Ham, I., and Ross, D.T. *Integrated Computer-Aided Manufacturing (ICAM) Task II Final Report*, Vol. 1, Group Technology Classification and Coding, USAF Technical Report AFML-TR-77-218, December 1977.
17. Japanese Society for Promotion of Machine Industry, *"Guide Book for Group Technology Implementation."* (Japanese), April 1979.
18. Thompson, A.R. "Establishing a Classification and Coding System." SME Technical Paper # MS76-276, 1976.
19. *CAM-I Training Material for CAPP*, CAM-I Automated Process Planning, Vol. 1, TM-77-AMP-01, published by Computer-Aided Manufacturing-International, Inc., Arlington, Texas, 1977.
20. Petrov, V.A. *Flowline Group Production Planning.* (English translation), London: Business Publications, Ltd., 1968.
21. Hitomi, K., and Ham, I. "Operations Scheduling for Group Technology Applications." *CIRP Annals*, 25 (August 1976), pp. 419–422
22. Hitomi, K., and Ham, I. "Group Scheduling Techniques for Multiproduction Multistage Manufacturing Systems." ASME Paper #76-WA/Prod-29; *ASME Transactions*, 99 (August 1977), pp. 759–765.
23. Hitomi, K., and Ham, I. "Machine Loading for Group Technology Applications." *CIRP Annals*, 26 (August 1977), pp. 279–281.
24. Hitomi, K., and Ham, I. "Machine Loading and Product-Mix Analysis for Group Technology." ASME Paper #77-WA/Prod21, *ASME Transactions*, 100 (August 1978): 370–374.
25. Ham, I., Hitomi, K., Nakajura, N., and Yoshida, T. "Optimal Group Scheduling and Machining—Speed Decision Under Due-Date Constraints." *ASME Transactions*, 101 (May 1979), pp. 128–134.
26. Taylor, J., and Ham, I. "The Use of a Micro Computer for Group Scheduling."

Proceedings of the IX North American Manufacturing Research Conference
1981, *SME Transactions*, published by Society of Manufacturing Engineers,
pp. 483–491, May 1981.
27.   Sato, N., Ignizio, J., and Ham, I. "Group Technology and Material Requirements Planning; An Integrated Methodology for Production Control." *CIRP
Annals*, 28 (August 1978), pp. 471–473.

3 PROCESS PLANNING FOR GROUP TECHNOLOGY

3.1 Essentials of Process Planning

Process planning is the decision making as to the production process through which raw materials are converted into products planned by product design, with a series of operations. This planning is interrelated with product design and layout planning. Information on technical specifications of products established by a product-design function is an important input to process planning. Layout planning requires information on the sequence of operations to manufacture each part or product, which is derived from process planning.

In general, process planning includes the following decision problems [1]:

1. **Process design (or work design).** This is a macroscopic decision making which determines an overall process route for converting raw materials into products. This includes flow-line analysis (analysis of work flow) and selection of work stations for each operation included in the work flow determined. A work flow for a product is usually determined with a process chart that indicates the sequence of operations composing multi-stage manufacturing. Then an appropriate

combination of work stations for performing operations included in the
work flow determined is selected from among several technologically
possible combinations of production facilities available and operative
human power.

2. **Operation design (or job design).** This is a microscopic decision
making as to the implementation of production. Specifically speaking,
this design decides the content of each operation in the work flow
determined by process design and the method of performing the
operations.

3.2 Basic Models of Process Planning

A work route for completing a product consists of multiple operations
(stages) such as turning, planing, drilling, finishing, and others, each of which
usually has several alternatives in terms of what type of machine is to be
used. Furthermore, several operations can be performed by using a single
machine, such as a machining center, that can perform a sequence of multiple
operations by automatically changing cutting tools. In general, there are
several alternative process routes for converting a piece of raw material into a
piece of product. From a process planning viewpoint, it is necessary to select
the one best process route (work flow) from among those alternatives under a
certain criterion such as minimum time, minimum cost, maximum productivity, and maximum profit. This decision is called "optimum process
planning," or "optimum routing analysis."

Consider a process planning problem that requires four stages of
operations—turning, planing, drilling, and finishing—to complete a product.
There are two, three, three, and two alternatives, respectively, for these four
operations. In addition, a machining center can be employed to perform both
planing and drilling operations. These alternative routings excluding technologically impossible ones can be represented in the form of a network, for
example, as shown in figure 3.1 [2]. In figure 3.1 arrows indicate operations
with definite work contents and production times (or costs). The present
problem is to select the one best work route from among 9 possible
alternative process patterns.

Clearly this problem is among a class of combinatorial problems. Since the
number of alternative process routes to be searched is limited, it is possible to
select the best one by complete enumeration, calculating total times (or
costs) for all possible process routes and then selecting a route with the least
time (or cost). This complete enumeration procedure is not an appropriate
method for large-scale process planning which includes a large number of

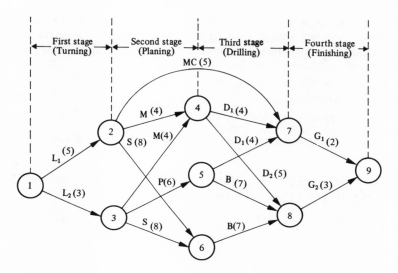

(Note) L: Lathe, B: Boring machine, G: Grinder, M: Milling machine

MC: Machining center, P: Planer, S: Shaper, D: Drilling machine

Figure 3.1. Network representation of alternative process routes

possible process routes. Dynamic programming is one of the effective methods for solving this type of problem with a less computational effort. "Dynamic programming" (DP) is a technique developed by R. Bellman for solving a special class of optimization problems called the multi-stage decision process [3]. The basic principle of dynamic programming is the "principle of optimality," which states that "an optimal policy has the property that whatever the initial state and the initial decision are, the remaining decisions must constitute an optimal policy with regard to the state resulting from the first decisions."

Example 3.1. Consider a process planning problem as shown in figure 3.1. An optimal work flow is determined by applying dynamic programming as follows:

Let $f(i)$ denote the minimum time required for performing all operations in the subroutes between node i and sink 9. Then, based on the principle of optimality, the following equation holds:

$$f(i) = \min_{j} (t_{ij} + f(j)) \qquad (3.1)$$

where t_{ij} is the processing time for the operation between node i and just next to node j. Since the total processing time of the optimal process route is given by $f(1)$, the optimal solution is determined by calculating $f(i)$, with the use of the recursive relation (equation 3.1), starting from $f(9)$ $(= 0)$ backwards until $f(1)$ is obtained. By using this backward calculation, an optimal route is determined as follows: Since

$$f(9) = 0, \text{ then}$$

$$f(8) = \min_{j=9}(t_{8j} + f(j)) = t_{89} + f(9) = 3 \ (8 - 9)$$

where $(i - j)$ signifies that the optimal route is from node i to node j. Similarly, $f(7) = 2 \ (7 - 9)$. Next,

$$f(6) = \min_{j=8}(t_{6j} + f(j))$$

$$= t_{68} + f(8)$$

$$= 7 + 3 = 10 \ (6 - 8)$$

Similarly, $f(5) = 6 \ (5 - 7)$ and $f(4) = 6 \ (4 - 7)$. Further,

$$f(3) = \min_{j=4,5,6}(t_{3j} + f(j))$$

$$= \min(4 + 6, \ 6 + 6, \ 8 + 10) = 10 \ (3 - 4)$$

and

$$f(2) = \min_{j=4,6,7}(t_{2j} + f(j))$$

$$= \min(4 + 6, \ 8 + 10, \ 5 + 2) = 7 \ (2 - 7)$$

Finally,

$$f(1) = \min_{j=2,3}(t_{1j} + f(j))$$

$$= \min(5 + 7, \ 3 + 10) = 12 \ (1 - 2)$$

Thus, an optimal process route minimizing the total processing time is determined as $1 - 2 - 7 - 9$ (5 hours for turning operation, 5 hours for machine center work, 2 hours for grinding operation), with the total processing time of 12 hours.

In addition to the above dynamic programming technique, the shortest path algorithm of network technique can be applied to solve optimum process planning problems [4].

3.3 Process Planning Models for Group Technology

In the previous section, a basic model of process planning for a single product item (or part) was mentioned by introducing network representation of several alternative work routes and selection of the best route by dynamic programming. In this case, no attention is paid to group technology applications. In this section, the concept of group technology is introduced to select the best process routes for producing a variety of products. To achieve the full advantages of group technology applications, this concept is employed in such management fields as process planning and scheduling.

When applying the group technology concept to process planning, alternative work routes to be searched should include ones for group processing in which several parts classified in the same part family are processed on the same sequence of machines with universal fixtures. Thus, process planning for group technology applications is to search alternative work routes for group processing in addition to ones for conventional processing.

There are two cases for process planning for group technology applications: one for a single part and the other for multiple parts.

1. **Process planning for a single part.** This single part is a member of a part family, in which the work route of each part has been determined. In addition to these conventional alternative work routes, there may be other alternative routes for group processing. It is relatively easy to deal with these additional work routes by simply adding them to the network representing the conventional work routes shown in figure 3.1.

   Suppose there is an alternative route of group processing for a turning operation between nodes 1 and 2, requiring 4 hours of processing time. This group-processing operation can be inserted in the conventional network of figure 3.1 by making a new node, 2′, and by introducing a dummy operation with a processing time of zero, as shown in figure 3.2. Thus, by applying dynamic programming to this network in the same way as in the case in figure 3.1, an optimal work flow can be determined as a route of $1 - 2' - 2 - 7 - 9$ with the total processing time of 11 hours.

2. **Process planning for multiple parts.** Process planning of multiple parts for group technology applications requires consideration of the

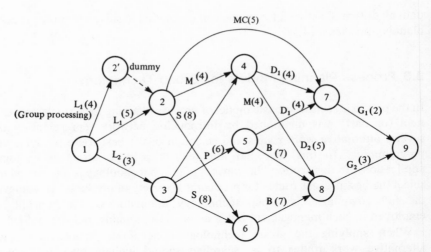

Figure 3.2. Network representation of alternative production process routes including group processing

possibility of group processing for several parts. Hence, alternative process routes to be considered include work routes for group processing as well as work routes for conventional processing. The process planning problem of this kind is also a class of combinatorial problems; an optimal solution can be selected from among a definite number of possible alternative process routes. This problem concerns how to enumerate—explicitly or implicitly—all possible process routes for all the parts concerned. One way to implicitly express all the possible routes is to represent them in the form of a network. To begin with, consider a case that the work flow for each part consists of a single operation. Alternative operations for completing three parts both in conventional processing and in group processing can be represented in the form of a network as shown in figure 3.3. In this network, an arrow between nodes 1 and 4 shows a work route that represents that parts 1 and 2 are processed on machine M_1 in group processing. Similarly, group processing on machine M_1 for all three parts is represented by an arrow between nodes 1 and 7. Other arrows in the network represent operations by conventional processing; each part is processed separately. An optimal work route consisting of production processes for three parts can be determined simultaneously by applying the dynamic

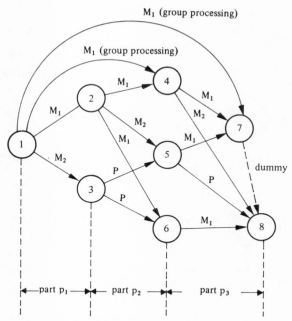

Figure 3.3. Network representation of alternative production process routes including group processing for turning operation of three parts

programming procedure, described earlier, to this network in the same way as for the problem concerning figure 3.1.

Next, consider a case that the work flow for each part consists of multiple operations. In this case, alternative process routes for the parts concerned also can be represented in the form of a network by combining in a series the network of work routes for the multiple operations. For example, alternative work routes for three parts having two operations can be represented by a network as shown in figure 3.4. In this figure, alternative work routes between nodes 1 and 6 represent the planing operation, and those between nodes 6 and 11 represent the drilling operation. Applying the dynamic programming technique to the network given by this figure, an optimal work route for completing three parts is determined as $1 - 4 - 6 - 9 - 11$ with the minimum total processing time of 29 hours. In this plan, parts 1 and 2 are processed on both machines M and D_1 in group processing, and part 3, on machines M and D_1 in conventional processing.

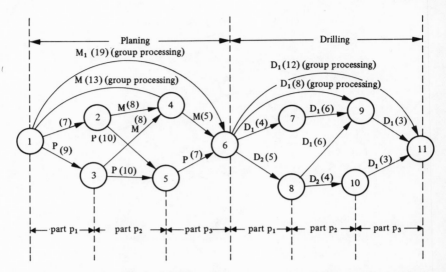

Figure 3.4.   Network representation of alternative production process
routes including group processing for two operations for completing
three parts

References

1.   Timms, H.L., and Pohlen, M.F. *The Production Function in Business—
     Decision Systems for Production and Operations Management*, 3rd ed.,
     Homewood, Illinois: Richard D. Irwin, 1970.
2.   Hitomi, K. *Manufacturing Systems Engineering*. London: Taylor & Francis
     Ltd., 1979.
3.   Bellman, R. *Dynamic Programming*. Princeton. N.J.: Princeton University
     Press, 1957.
4.   Whitehouse, G.E. *Systems Analysis and Decision Using Network Techniques*.
     Englewood Cliffs, N.J.: Prentice-Hall, 1974.

4 PRODUCTION PLANNING FOR GROUP TECHNOLOGY APPLICATIONS

4.1 Essentials of Production Planning

→In order to obtain desirable profit and survive as long as possible, manufacturing firms should make their best efforts to establish various planning activities in different levels of the management hierarchy. Planning activities are usually classified into three levels: strategic, managerial, and operational. Production planning—mostly concerned with managerial and operational planning—is one of the most important functions in production management planning activities.

Production planning is a function that determines the kinds of product items and the quantities to be produced in the specified time period, subject to the production capacity including human power and the due dates given to order or the deadlines given for production for stock replenishment. This aggregate planning is usually established based on demand forecasting, which is a function of estimating what kinds of product items and how many are required in the market. It is also based on product planning, one of the basic planning functions in strategic planning, which decides on new types of products to be created in the future. Production planning is definitely connected with other operational planning activities such as machine loading, production scheduling, and process planning, giving the important information necessary to make proper plans for these production activities. Production planning includes the following decision problems [1]:

1. **Optimal product mix.** This determines an optimal combination of kinds of product items to be produced with the existing production capacity.
2. **Requirement analysis.** This determines, in a specified time period, the quantities for the products which are decided to be produced by optimal product mix.
3. **Lot-size analysis.** This determines the optimal production quantities (or economic order quantity, EOQ) in intermittent production where the demand rate for a product is small compared with the production rate for the product.
4. **Production smoothing.** This determines, in some time periods, the production quantities of product items of fluctuated demand over a time period so that the level of production is evened up.

4.2 Basic Models of Production Planning

4.2.1 Linear-Programming Model for Product-Mix and Requirement Analysis

Linear programming (LP) [2], one of the effective mathematical optimization techniques, is most frequently employed in production planning.

Suppose n kinds of products (or parts) are produced with m kinds of production resources, such as raw materials, machines, labor forces, and capital. Let a_{ij} denote the units of resource i $(i = 1, 2, \ldots, m)$ which are required to produce a unit of product j, from which c_j units of profit are gained. There are only b_i available units of resource i. The problem is to determine optimal production quantities such that the total profit is maximized, subject to resource constraints.

By denoting the amount of product j $(j = 1, 2, \ldots, n)$ by x_j, the decision problem is expressed as a linear programming model as follows:
Maximize

$$z = \sum_{j=1}^{n} c_j x_j \qquad (4.1)$$

subject to

$$\sum_{j=1}^{n} a_{ij} x_j \leq b_i \ (i = 1, 2, \ldots, m) \qquad (4.2)$$

$$x_j \geq 0 \quad (j = 1, 2, \ldots, n) \qquad (4.3)$$

In the above formulation, the first expression is the objective function (total profit) to be maximized, the second equation indicates the constraints for resource limitation, and the last equation is nonnegative requirements showing production of zero or positive quantities.

Depending on the problem defined, the objective function may be minimized and/or the constraints may also be stated with equal-to signs ($= 0$) or greater-than or equal-to signs (≥ 0).

The linear programming formulation requires the following three basic conditions:

1. proportionality of production resources required and associated profit to production quantities for each activity
2. additivity of production resources required and profit
3. divisibility of production quantities (continuous decision variables)

4.2.2 Lot-Size Analysis

When the production rate of a product item is large compared with the demand rate for the item, continuous production will make the inventory of the item increase. To avoid this, the product item demanded is manufactured periodically in a quantity that will meet the demand for some time periods until the next production is run. This periodical production makes it possible to manufacture other product items by making use of the time interval between two production runs for the first product. This type of production is called "intermittent production," or "lot (or batch) production."

The problem involved in lot production is to determine the ordering quantities (called "lot sizes") in a production run and production cycle for each product item. In lot-size analysis, the minimization of the total variable cost consisting of inventory-holding cost and setup cost is usually employed as the criterion of determining optimal lot sizes and production cycle.

Consider a lot-sizing problem for a single product item. Let production rate (pcs/day) and demand rate (pcs/day) be p and r, respectively, and $p > r$. Furthermore, let I and U be inventory-holding cost per unit piece of product per time unit and setup cost per cycle or lot, respectively. During the production period, W, in a production cycle, T, the product inventory increases up to a maximum level, Q', at a constant rate of $(p - r)$. During the nonproduction period, $(T - W)$, the inventory decreases down to zero at a constant rate of r. This pattern of inventory change is shown in figure 4.1.

It is clear from figure 4.1 that the average inventory level over a production

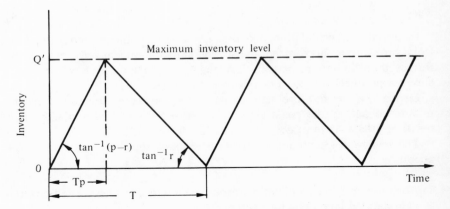

Figure 4.1.   Inventory-time chart of a single product in lot production

cycle is $Q'/2$. Hence, the inventory-holding cost per lot is $IQ'T/2$; thus, the inventory-holding cost per unit is $IQ'T/(2Q)$. On the other hand, the setup cost per unit is given by U/Q. Thus, for the total variable cost per unit, the objective function to be minimized is:

$$C = \frac{U}{Q} + \frac{IQ'T}{2Q} \tag{4.4}$$

It is clear from figure 4.1 that $T = Q/r$ and $Q' = (p - r)T_p = (p - r)Q/p$. From equation 4.4 and these relations, we obtain the following equation:

$$C = \frac{U}{Q} + \frac{I}{2r}\left(1 - \frac{r}{p}\right)Q \tag{4.5}$$

The optimal (or economic) lot size is determined by differentiating the above equation with respect to Q and setting it at zero as follows:

$$Q^* = \sqrt{\frac{2rU}{\left(1 - \frac{r}{p}\right)I}} \tag{4.6}$$

Then, the optimal production cycle is obtained as:

$$T^* = \frac{Q^*}{r} = \sqrt{\frac{2U}{\left(1 - \frac{r}{p}\right)rI}} \tag{4.7}$$

The production time for this optimal plan is:

$$W^* = \frac{Q^*}{p} = \frac{1}{p}\sqrt{\frac{2rU}{\left(1 - \frac{r}{p}\right)I}} \qquad (4.8)$$

In general, the total variable cost curve is shallow near the optimal lot size; therefore, the curve is relatively insensitive to deviation from that lot size (refer to figure 4.2).

Example 4.1. Consider a problem for lot-size analysis, given the following data: production rate $(p) = 200$ (pcs/day); demand rate $(r) = 50$ (pcs/day); setup cost $(U) = 3000$ ($/lot); and inventory-holding cost $(I) = 1$ ($/pc/day).
Then the optimal lot size is:

$$Q^* = \sqrt{\frac{2 \times 50 \times 3000}{1 \times \left(1 - \frac{50}{200}\right)}} \doteq 632 \text{ (pcs)} \qquad (4.9)$$

The optimal production cycle and the optimal production period are, respectively:

$$T^* = \frac{Q^*}{r} = \frac{632.4}{50} = 12.6 \text{ (days)} \qquad (4.10)$$

$$W^* = \frac{Q^*}{p} = \frac{632.4}{200} = 3.2 \text{ (days)} \qquad (4.11)$$

The curve for the total variable cost for this example is given in figure 4.2.

In practical situations, multiple product items are assigned to one facility for lot production. The lot-sizing problem for multiple product items is a challenging one when an optimal solution is required in the true sense of the word *optimal*. However, if it is assumed that all product items to be produced have the same production cycle and each is manufactured once in the common production cycle, the problem is a relatively easy one. Decisions to be made in the present problem are to determine the optimal production cycle and the economic lot sizes for all the items. A lot-size analysis for multiple items is performed under the assumption as follows: In the case of multiple items, the total variable cost per unit piece of product items is meaningless as the objective function to be minimized. Thus, time is employed as the common unit in estimating total variable cost.

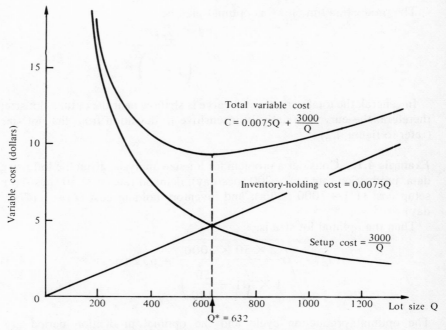

Figure 4.2. Inventory-holding cost, setup cost, and total variable cost per unit

Then, the total variable cost per unit time is expressed as a function of production cycle, T, as follows:

$$C = \sum_{i=1}^{n} \left[\frac{U_i}{T} + \frac{r_i I_i}{2} \left(1 - \frac{r_i}{p_i} \right) T \right] \qquad (4.12)$$

where n is the number of product items to be produced and a subscript i is used for the previous nomenclature to indicate the association with product item i.

The optimal production cycle, the same for all n product items, is determined by differentiating the above equation with regard to T and setting it at zero as follows:

$$T^* = \sqrt{\frac{2 \sum\limits_{i=1}^{n} U_i}{\sum\limits_{i=1}^{n} \left(1 - \dfrac{r_i}{p_i} \right) r_i I_i}} \qquad (4.13)$$

Thus, the economic lot sizes for all product items are:

$$Q_i^* = r_i T^* = r_i \sqrt{\dfrac{2\sum\limits_{j=1}^{n} U_j}{\sum\limits_{j=1}^{n}\left(1 - \dfrac{r_j}{p_j}\right) r_j I_j}} \quad (i = 1, 2, \ldots, n) \tag{4.14}$$

Since the sum of the total production time needed to produce all the product items and the total setup time is required to be less than the production cycle obtained, the following equation must hold for feasibility of the solution:

$$\sum_{i=1}^{n}\left(S_i + \frac{Q_i^*}{p_i}\right) \leq T^* \tag{4.15}$$

where S_i is setup time necessary for product item i.

4.3 Production Planning Models for Group Technology

Basic production planning models mentioned in the previous section are extended in this section by applying the concept of group technology. One of the most prominent advantages of applying group technology to production is reduction of setup time (a time necessary to make machines ready to work), which plays a critical role in production planning.

Based on this principle, a basic production planning model for group technology applications can be constructed under the following assumptions:

1. Jobs (tasks of converting materials into finished parts or products) are to be processed on a production system that consists of m machines.
2. Jobs to be processed are classified into several groups (part or product families), based on the group technology concept.
3. Group processing time required for completing a group of parts consists of group setup time and the sum of job processing times for jobs contained in that group.
4. Basic conditions to be satisfied in employing linear programming for production planning are satisfied.

In formulating a group production planning, let $J_{i\xi}$ $(i = 1, 2, \ldots, N, \xi = 1, 2, \ldots, n_i)$ denote ξth job in group $G_i(i = 1, 2, \ldots, N)$ and $r_{i\xi}$ and $u_{i\xi}^k$ denote the unit profit of $J_{i\xi}$ and the unit processing time on machine M_k of $J_{i\xi}$. In addition, let S_i^k denote the group setup time on M_k for G_i. Merely b_k time units are available for M_k.

The problem to be solved is to determine optimal production quantities so as to maximize the total profit, subject to time (resource) constraints. Denoting the production amount of part $J_{i\xi}$ by $x_{i\xi}$, this decision problem is formulated as:

Maximize

$$z = \sum_{i=1}^{N} \sum_{\xi=1}^{n_i} r_{i\xi} x_{i\xi} \qquad (4.16)$$

subject to

$$\sum_{i=1}^{N} \left(S_i^k X_i + \sum_{\xi=1}^{n_i} u_{i\xi}^k x_{i\xi} \right) \le b_k \qquad (4.17)$$

$$x_{i\xi} \ge 0 \ (i = 1, 2, \ldots N, \ \xi = 1, 2, \ldots, n_i) \qquad (4.18)$$

where

$$X_i = \begin{cases} 0, \text{ if } \sum_{\xi=1}^{n_i} x_{i\xi} = 0 \\[2em] 1, \text{ if } \sum_{\xi=1}^{n_i} x_{i\xi} > 0 \end{cases} \qquad (4.19)$$

The above problem differs from a typical linear programming problem in that 0-1 type variables which indicate whether any part of each group is produced or not are introduced in the time constraints to incorporate the feature of group setup time into the model. However, the solution to this problem is not an easy one; it is different from a linear programming problem. A primitive, and inefficient, method for solving this problem is to solve all linear programming problems for all combinations of 0-1 type variables. For a problem of N groups involved, the number of combinations to be considered is 2^N. Since the problem includes integer variables in its model by only the number of groups, not the number of jobs, use of this complete-enumeration method does not necessarily appear to be impossible for solving the problem of moderate size.

Example 4.2. Consider a five-job, two-group production planning problem, with basic data as given in table 4.1.

Table 4.1. Production Data for Example 4.3

Group		G_1			G_2			
Job		J_{11}	J_{12}		J_{21}	J_{22}	J_{23}	
Group setup time/ Job processing time	S_1^k	u_{11}^k	u_{12}^k	S_2^k	u_{21}^k	u_{22}^k	u_{23}^k	Time available
Machine M_1	10	5	8	20	3	2	6	200
Machine M_2	25	7	4	10	2	5	4	150
Machine M_3	15	4	5	20	4	7	5	180
Profit		3	7		4	2	5	

Applying the formulation of equations 4.16, 4.17, 4.18, and 4.19 to this example, we obtain the following problem:
Maximize

$$z = 3x_{11} + 7x_{12} + 4x_{21} + 2x_{22} + 5x_{23} \qquad (4.20)$$

subject to

$$\left.\begin{array}{l} 10X_1 + 5x_{11} + 8x_{12} + 20X_2 + 3x_{21} + 2x_{22} + 6x_{23} \leq 200 \\ 25X_1 + 7x_{11} + 4x_{12} + 10X_2 + 2x_{21} + 5x_{22} + 4x_{23} \leq 150 \\ 15X_1 + 4x_{11} + 5x_{12} + 20X_2 + 4x_{21} + 7x_{22} + 5x_{23} \leq 180 \end{array}\right\} \qquad (4.21)$$

$$x_{11} \geq 0,\ x_{12} \geq 0,\ x_{21} \geq 0,\ x_{22} \geq 0,\ x_{23} \geq 0 \qquad (4.22)$$

where

$$\left.\begin{array}{l} X_1 = \begin{cases} 0, & \text{if } x_{11} + x_{12} = 0 \\ 1, & \text{if } x_{11} + x_{12} > 0 \end{cases} \\[2em] X_2 = \begin{cases} 0, & \text{if } x_{21} + x_{22} + x_{23} = 0 \\ 1, & \text{if } x_{21} + x_{22} + x_{23} > 0 \end{cases} \end{array}\right\} \qquad (4.23)$$

Since two groups are included in this problem, there exist four possible combinations of 0-1 type variables, that is $(X_1, X_2) = \{(1, 1), (1, 0), (0, 1)$

$(0, 0)$}. Among these four combinations, the linear programming problems for the first three deserve to be solved. The time constraints for each of the three combinations of 0-1 type variables as follows:

(a) For combination of $(1, 1)$,

$$\left.\begin{array}{l} 5x_{11} + 8x_{12} + 3x_{21} + 2x_{22} + 6x_{23} \leq 170 \\ 7x_{11} + 4x_{12} + 2x_{21} + 5x_{22} + 4x_{23} \leq 115 \\ 4x_{11} + 5x_{12} + 4x_{21} + 7x_{22} + 5x_{23} \leq 145 \end{array}\right\} \quad (4.24)$$

(b) For combination of $(1, 0)$,

$$\left.\begin{array}{l} 5x_{11} + 8x_{12} \leq 190 \\ 7x_{11} + 4x_{12} \leq 125 \\ 4x_{11} + 5x_{12} \leq 165 \end{array}\right\} \quad (4.25)$$

(c) For combination of $(0, 1)$,

$$\left.\begin{array}{l} 3x_{21} + 2x_{22} + 6x_{23} \leq 180 \\ 2x_{21} + 5x_{22} + 4x_{23} \leq 140 \\ 4x_{21} + 7x_{22} + 5x_{23} \leq 160 \end{array}\right\} \quad (4.26)$$

By solving the linear programming problem with the objective function of equation 4.20, each of the above constraints (a), (b), and (c) and nonnegative requirements of equation 4.22, we obtain solutions as shown in table 4.2. From this table, the optimal production quantities for five jobs are decided as $(x_{11}, x_{12}, x_{21}, x_{22}, x_{23}) = (0, 0, 28, 0, 16)$, which yields a maximum total profit of 192.

4.4 Lot-Size Analysis for Group Technology

In multi-product small-lot-sized production, as was stated in previous chapters, parts are often classified into several families, or groups of parts. In such a case, a production facility may be used to produce parts that fall into two or more families. This situation makes lot-size analysis more formidable to treat and strictly optimal to solve. However, by introducing a rather strict assumption that all parts included in all the families to be produced have the same production cycle and each part is manufactured once each production cycle, lot-sizing problems of producing several families on a facility can be treated in much the same way as in the conventional case of section 4.2.

Consider a single facility lot-sizing problem of N groups, (part or product

Table 4.2. Solutions for three linear programming problems

Combination of (X_1, X_2)	Optimal Production Quantities					Maximum Profit
	J_{11}	J_{12}	J_{21}	J_{22}	J_{23}	
(1, 1)	0	0	24	0	16.3	177.7
(1, 0)	0	23.6	0	0	0	165
(0, 1)	0	0	28	0	16	192

families), each consisting of n_i parts ($i = 1, 2, \ldots, N$). Let production rate (pcs/day) and demand rate (pcs/day) for part ξ of group i (G_i) be $p_{i\xi}$ and $r_{i\xi}$, respectively. Furthermore, let $I_{i\xi}$ be inventory-holding cost per unit piece of part ξ of group G_i per time unit. The intergroup setup cost (or group setup cost) for G_i and the intragroup setup cost (or job setup cost) for part ξ of G_i are given by U_i and $u_{i\xi}$, respectively.

Then, the total setup cost per production cycle is given by:

$$C_1 = \sum_{i=1}^{N} \left(U_i + \sum_{\xi=1}^{n_i} u_{i\xi} \right) \qquad (4.27)$$

After denoting the maximum inventory level for part ξ of G_i by $Q'_{i\xi}$, the total inventory-holding cost per production cycle is given by:

$$C_2 = \sum_{i=1}^{N} \sum_{\xi=1}^{n_i} \frac{I_{i\xi} Q'_{i\xi} T}{2} = \frac{1}{2} \sum_{i=1}^{N} \sum_{\xi=1}^{n_i} \left(1 - \frac{r_{i\xi}}{p_{i\xi}} \right) r_{i\xi} I_{i\xi} T^2 \qquad (4.28)$$

since $Q'_{i\xi} = (p_{i\xi} - r_{i\xi}) r_{i\xi} T / p_{i\xi}$

Thus, the total variable cost per unit time is expressed as a function of production cycle, T, as follows:

$$C = (C_1 + C_2)/T$$

$$= \frac{1}{T} \sum_{i=1}^{N} \left(U_i + \sum_{\xi=1}^{n_i} u_{i\xi} \right) + \frac{1}{2} \sum_{i=1}^{N} \sum_{\xi=1}^{n_i} \left(1 - \frac{r_{i\xi}}{p_{i\xi}} \right) r_{i\xi} I_{i\xi} T \qquad (4.29)$$

The optimal production cycle is easily determined from this equation as:

$$T^* = \sqrt{2 \sum_{i=1}^{N} \left(U_i + \sum_{\xi=1}^{n_i} u_{i\xi} \right) \Big/ \sum_{i=1}^{N} \sum_{\xi=1}^{n_i} \left(1 - \frac{r_{i\xi}}{p_{i\xi}} \right) r_{i\xi} I_{i\xi}} \qquad (4.30)$$

The economic lot sizes are:

$$Q_{i\xi}^* = r_{i\xi} \sqrt{2 \sum_{j=1}^{N} \left(U_j + \sum_{\eta=1}^{n_j} u_{j\eta} \right) \bigg/ \left\{ \sum_{j=1}^{N} \sum_{\eta=1}^{n_j} \left(1 - \frac{r_{j\eta}}{p_{j\eta}} \right) r_{j\eta} I_{j\eta} \right\}}$$

$$(i = 1,2, \ldots N, \; \xi = 1,2, \ldots n_i) \qquad (4.31)$$

The feasibility of the solution obtained requires the following condition:

$$\sum_{i=1}^{N} \left(S_i + \sum_{\xi=1}^{n_i} s_{i\xi} \right) + \sum_{i=1}^{N} \sum_{\xi=1}^{n_i} \frac{Q_{i\xi}^*}{p_{i\xi}} \leq T^* \qquad (4.32)$$

where S_i and $s_{i\xi}$ are intergroup setup time (or group setup time) for G_i and intragroup setup time (or job setup time) for part ξ in G_i, respectively.

Since the intragroup setup cost is usually small relative to the intergroup setup cost, it is reasonable that the intragroup setup cost is assumed to be zero for all parts. In that case ($u_{i\xi} = 0$), the optimal production cycle and the economic lot sizes are respectively given by:

$$T^* = \sqrt{2 \sum_{i=1}^{N} U_i \bigg/ \left\{ \sum_{i=1}^{N} \sum_{\xi=1}^{n_i} \left(1 - \frac{r_{i\xi}}{p_{i\xi}} \right) r_{i\xi} I_{i\xi} \right\}} \qquad (4.33)$$

$$Q_{i\xi}^* = r_{i\xi} \sqrt{2 \sum_{j=1}^{N} U_j \bigg/ \left\{ \sum_{j=1}^{N} \sum_{\eta=1}^{n_j} \left(1 - \frac{r_{j\eta}}{p_{j\eta}} \right) r_{j\eta} I_{j\eta} \right\}} \qquad (4.34)$$

$$(i = 1, 2, \ldots, N, \; \xi = 1, 2, \ldots, n_i)$$

Example 4.3. Consider a lot-sizing problem for group technology applications, with basic data as shown by table 4.3.

From equation 4.33, the optimal production cycle is:

$$T^* = \sqrt{2 \times \{350 + 400 + (5 + 8) + (7 + 10 + 5)\} \bigg/ \left\{ \left(1 - \frac{10}{150} \right) \times \right.}$$

$$10 \times 0.01 + \left(1 - \frac{30}{200} \right) \times 30 \times 0.01 + \left(1 - \frac{15}{100} \right) \times 15 \times$$

$$0.005 + \left(1 - \frac{25}{180} \right) \times 25 \times 0.005 + \left(1 - \frac{20}{120} \right) \times 20 \times$$

$$\left. 0.008 \right\}$$

$$= 49.0 \text{ (days)} \qquad (4.35)$$

Table 4.3 Basic data for lot-sizing problem for group technology applications

Group (Family)	G_1		G_2		
Part	1	2	1	2	3
Production rate per day	150	200	100	180	120
Consumption rate per day	10	30	15	25	20
Inventory holding cost ($ per unit per day)	0.01	0.01	0.005	0.005	0.008
Intergroup setup cost ($/cycle)	5	8	7	10	5
Intragroup setup time (day/cycle)	0.9	0.2	0.2	0.1	0.3
Intergroup setup cost ($/cycle)	350		400		
Intergroup setup time (day/cycle)	2		3		

Thus, the economic lot size for each part is determined by using the relation of $Q_i^* = r_{i\xi} T^*$ as $(Q_{11}^*, Q_{12}^*, Q_{21}^*, Q_{22}^*, Q_{23}^*) = (490, 1470, 735, 1225, 980)$. The production time for each part is computed by $W_{i\xi}^* = Q_{i\xi}^*/p_{i\xi}$ as $(W_{11}^*, W_{12}^*, W_{21}^*, W_{22}^*, W_{23}^*) = (3.3, 7.4, 7.4, 6.8, 8.2)$. This plan is feasible since the sum of the total production time ($= 33.1$) and the total setup time ($= 5.9$) is less than the production cycle obtained ($= 49.0$), satisfying equation 4.32.

Besides the above lot-sizing model for group technology applications requiring a rather strict assumption, a more practical problem has been considered that is based on the disaggregation of the aggregate plan determined by production planning [3].

References

1. Hitomi, K. *Manufacturing Systems Engineering*. London: Taylor & Francis, pp. 97–98, 1979.
2. Dantzig, G.B. *Linear Programming and Extensions*. Princeton, N.J.: Princeton University Press, 1963.
3. Dedworth, D.D., and Bailey, J.E. *Integrated Production Control Systems*. New York: John Wiley, pp. 161–166, 1982.

5 MACHINE LOADING FOR GROUP TECHNOLOGY

5.1 Essentials of Machine Loading

After product items and their quantities to be manufactured are determined by production planning, the next problem to be solved in production management is that of allocating the work loads to the existing production facilities for manufacturing these products. In general, capacities of the facilities including human power are not infinite. Therefore, in order to actually perform production activities according to the production plan established, it is essential to adjust the work load for each of the facilities and workers in every time period to not exceed the capacity. This decision is called "machine loading."

5.2 Basic Models of Machine Loading

The machine loading problem is basically that of allocating jobs to be processed to the existing machines such that the work load for each of the machines does not exceed its limited production capacity. In the field of operations research and management science, this machine loading problem is formulated as an assignment problem or simply a loading problem. Several useful procedures have been developed for solving these problems.

5.2.1 Assignment Problem

The basic assignment problem can be stated as follows: There are n jobs to be processed, each of which can be processed on any of n machines at varying costs. A job must be assigned only one machine and, conversely, a machine must perform only one job. Let c_{ij} denote the processing cost of assigning job J_i to machine M_j. 0-1 type variables, x_{ij}, are introduced, such that $x_{ij} = 1$ when J_i is assigned to M_j, and $x_{ij} = 0$ when J_i is not assigned to M_j.

The assignment problem can be formulated as follows:
Minimize

$$z = \sum_{i=1}^{n} \sum_{j=1}^{n} c_{ij} x_{ij} \tag{5.1}$$

Subject to

$$\left.\begin{array}{l} \sum_{i=1}^{n} x_{ij} = 1 \quad (j = 1, 2, \ldots, n) \\[2mm] \sum_{j=1}^{n} x_{ij} = 1 \quad (i = 1, 2, \ldots, n) \end{array}\right\} \tag{5.2}$$

In the above formulation, the two constraints assure that a job is assigned to only one machine and, conversely, a machine can perform only one job. The objective of this problem is to find the best assignment of jobs to machines under the minimum-cost criterion. A variety of procedures for solving the assignment problem have been developed. The primitive method is complete enumeration of all possible assignments. Principally, there will be a definite possible solution; that is, $n! \ (= n \times (n-1) \times \ldots \times 1)$. One could conceivably identify all such alternatives and then choose a solution having the lowest cost. However, it is practically difficult to find an optimal solution in the case of large numbers of jobs and machines.

The assignment problem is clearly a problem of integer linear programming; it can be solved by the general solution procedure of integer linear programming. However, this method is not a good one for the assignment problem since it cannot exploit the structure of an assignment cost matrix.

The Hungarian method [1] is known as the most efficient technique for finding an optimal assignment. This method takes full advantage of the structure of the assignment cost matrix. The Hungarian method consists of the following steps:

Step 1. Reduce each row of assignment cost matrix by subtracting the smallest entry in that row from every entry in that row. Then reduce each column of the cost matrix by subtracting the smallest entry in that column from each entry in that column.

Step 2. Find the maximal assignment that has zero entries in the cost matrix, as many as possible. If this maximal assignment is an optimal solution, then stop. Otherwise, proceed to the next step.

Step 3. Cover, with horizontal or vertical lines, each row and column that contains a zero entry such that the number of the covering lines is the minimum. Subtract the smallest entry in the uncovered positions from all uncovered entries and add it to all entries where the covering lines intersect. Return to step 2.

Example 5.1. Consider a problem of assigning 5 jobs to 5 machines, which has a cost matrix as shown in table 5.1.

Step 1. Reduce the cost matrix by subtracting the smallest number in each row from each entry in that row, which results in table 5.2 (a). For example, the smallest number in the first row of table 5.1 is 4. Subtracting it from every entry in the first row transforms that row into 4, 5, 0, 7, and 1. Then reduce each column in the same way, which results in table 5.2 (b).

Step 2. The maximum assignment shown in circles in table 5.2 (b) is not optimal, since the number of zero entries in it is less than the number of rows.

Step 3. Covering lines are shown in table 5.2 (c). The smallest entry in the uncovered positions is 2 (the third row and the second column). Subtracting 2 from all uncovered entries and adding it to the intersection of the covering lines yields table 5.2 (d). Return to step 2.

Step 2. The maximum assignment, which is shown in circles in table 5.2 (d) $(x_{13} = x_{25} = x_{32} = x_{44} = x_{51} = 1)$ is optimal. The total cost of this assignment is $4 + 6 + 5 + 6 + 3 = 24$ (dollars).

Table 5.1.   Assignment problem of five jobs to five machines (units: dollars)

Job	\multicolumn{5}{c}{Machine}
	M_1	M_2	M_3	M_4	M_5
J_1	8	9	4	11	5
J_2	6	10	7	5	6
J_3	3	5	8	9	10
J_4	7	6	9	6	8
J_5	3	8	5	7	9

Table 5.2. Solution procedure of assignment
problem (table 5.1)

(a)

			Machine		
Job	M_1	M_2	M_3	M_4	M_5
J_1	4	5	0	7	1
J_2	1	5	2	0	1
J_3	0	2	5	6	7
J_4	1	0	3	0	2
J_5	0	5	2	4	6

(b)

			Machine		
Job	M_1	M_2	M_3	M_4	M_5
J_1	4	5	⓪	7	0
J_2	1	5	2	⓪	0
J_3	⓪	2	5	6	5
J_4	1	⓪	3	0	1
J_5	0	5	2	4	5

(c)

			Machine		
Job	M_1	M_2	M_3	M_4	M_5
J_1	4̶	5̶	0̶	7̶	0̶
J_2		5̶	2̶	0̶	0̶
J_3	0	2	5	6	5
J_4		0̶	3̶	0̶	1̶
J_5	0	5	3	4	5

(d)

			Machine		
Job	M_1	M_2	M_3	M_4	M_5
J_1	6	5	⓪	7	0
J_2	3	5	2	0	⓪
J_3	0	⓪	3	4	3
J_4	3	0	3	⓪	1
J_5	⓪	3	1	2	3

The above basic assignment problem has a balanced matrix; that is, the number of rows (jobs) equals the number of columns (machines). In some cases, the number of jobs does not equal the number of machines. In those cases, the imbalance is resolved by adding enough dummy rows or columns at cost zero to the cost matrix.

There is another extension of the basic assignment model. The basic assignment model assumes that there is a one-to-one correspondence between jobs and machines. In some cases, some jobs can be assigned to more than one machine. The model for this situation is known as the generalized assignment problem. The generalized assignment problem is formulated as follows:

There are n jobs to be processed, each of which can be processed on any of m machines with limited available times of d_j $(j = 1, 2, \ldots, m)$ at varying processing times a_{ij} $(i = 1, 2, \ldots, n, j = 1, 2, \ldots, m)$. The cost assigning job J_i to machine M_j is c_{ij}. A job must be assigned to only one machine; however, a machine can perform more than one job as long as the machine time is available. The problem is then formulated as follows:

Minimize

$$z = \sum_{i=1}^{n} \sum_{j=1}^{m} c_{ij} x_{ij} \tag{5.3}$$

subject to

$$\left.\begin{array}{l} \sum_{i=1}^{n} a_{ij} x_{ij} \leq d_j \quad (j = 1, 2, \ldots, m) \\[2ex] \sum_{j=1}^{n} x_{ij} = 1 \quad (i = 1, 2 \ldots, n) \\[2ex] x_{ij} = \begin{cases} 1, & \text{if } J_i \text{ is assigned to } M_j \\ 0, & \text{otherwise} \end{cases} \end{array}\right\} \tag{5.4}$$

The branch-and-bound algorithm for solving this problem has been developed [2].

5.2.2 Loading Problem

The loading problem is generally defined as the allocation of given items with known volumes to boxes with limited capacities, so as to maximize a given measure of performance. Therefore, the loading problem is considered to be a variation of the generalized assignment problem. When items and boxes are replaced by jobs and machines, respectively, the above loading problem is regarded as the machine loading problem. A typical machine loading problem is formulated as follows: n jobs are to be processed on m machines with limited available time d_j ($j = 1, 2, \ldots, m$). Let a_{ij} ($i = 1, 2, \ldots, n$, $j = 1, 2, \ldots, m$) denote the processing time of job J_i ($i = 1, 2 \ldots, n$) on machine M_j ($j = 1, 2, \ldots, m$) and r_i ($i = 1, 2, \ldots, n$) denote the profit obtained by producing J_i. The problem is to determine the optimal product-mix (optimal kinds of jobs) within the available machine times, so as to maximize the total profit.

Introducing 0-1 type variables, x_i ($i = 1, 2, \ldots, n$), that is $x_i = 1$ when J_i is selected to be produced, and $x_i = 0$ when J_i is rejected and not produced, the following constraints must be satisfied, since the given machine time available for each machine is limited to d_j.

$$\sum_{i=1}^{n} a_{ij}x_i \leq d_j \quad (j = 1, 2, \ldots, m) \tag{5.5}$$

$$x_i = \begin{cases} 1, \text{ if } J_i \text{ is selected to produce} \\ 0, \text{ otherwise} \end{cases}$$

The total profit, the objective function to be maximized is:

$$z = \sum_{i=1}^{n} r_i x_i \tag{5.6}$$

The machine loading problem is now formulated so as to maximize equation 5.6 subject to equation 5.5.

It is clear that the above problem is a typical 0–1 type linear programming problem. Several general solution procedures, such as the branch-and-bound approach and Balas' additive algorithm [3], can be applied to solving the problem.

In the case of a single machine ($a_{ij} = a_i$), the above machine loading problem is the so-called knapsack problem. Of course, the knapsack problem can be solved by the solution techniques for solving general integer linear programming problems. However, for solving the knapsack problem simply, it is advantageous to use a heuristic procedure that incorporates the concept of marginal profit (that is, profit per unit time; r_i/a_i for J_i). The heuristic procedure is as follows [4]:

Step 1. Compute the marginal profit for each job.

Step 2. Select jobs in nondecreasing order of the marginal profit obtained until the total processing time of the selected jobs exceeds the machine time available.

Example 5.2 Consider a knapsack problem of processing 5 jobs on a machine with the available time of 40 hours. The profits and processing times of 5 jobs are given in table 5.3. This knapsack problem is formulated as follows:

Maximize

$$z = 4x_1 + 3x_2 + 11x_3 + 7x_4 + 2x_5$$

subject to

$$12x_1 + 8x_2 + 28x_3 + 20x_4 + 5x_5 \leq 40$$

$$x_1, x_2, x_3, x_4, x_5 = 0 \text{ or } 1$$

Unit marginal profits for these jobs are computed as $4/12 = 0.33$ for J_1, $3/8 = 0.38$ for J_2, $11/28 = 0.39$ for J_3, $7/20 = 0.35$ for J_4, and $2/5 = 0.4$ for J_5. Thus, at first J_5 having the largest marginal profit is selected. The slack time available is $40 - 5 = 35$ hours. Then J_3 having the second largest marginal profit is selected. The slack time available is $40 - 5 - 28 = 7$ hours; hence, none of the remaining jobs can be selected anymore to produce. The total profit for this solution is 13 dollars.

This heuristic procedure easily gives a good solution, but it does not always give an optimal one. As a matter of fact, the solution obtained by the above example is not an optimal one. The optimal solution is clearly $x_1 = x_2 = x_4 = 1$, $x_3 = x_5 = 0$, and $z_{max} = 14$.

5.3 Group Machine Loading Models

5.3.1 Basic Models of Group Machine Loading

In the previous section, basic machine loading models were explained. In this section, machine loading problems for group technology applications are considered. One of the advantages of applying group technology to machine loading problems is the reduction of setup times. Parts, each of which belongs

Table 5.3   Basic data for knapsack problem

Job	J_1	J_2	J_3	J_4	J_5
Profit ($)	4	3	11	7	2
Processing time (h)	12	8	28	20	5

to one of the groups classified by the group technology concept, are to be assigned to machines. In this situation, two kinds of setup times for processing jobs are required. One is job setup time for each part, and the other, group setup time for each group consisting of several parts. Job setup time is needed whenever every part is assigned to be processed on a machine, while group setup time is needed only when the first part of a new group is assigned to a machine and is not needed when other parts of the same group are successively assigned to that machine. Therefore, in modeling a machine loading problem with group technology applications, it is required to incorporate both the setup times for groups and jobs. The above consideration leads to the following group machine loading model.

The fundamental assumptions of a group machine loading model are as follows:

1. Parts (or jobs) are to be processed on a production system which consists of K machines.
2. Jobs are classified into several groups.
3. Group processing time required for completion of a group consists of group setup time and the sum of job processing times for jobs contained in that group.
4. Job processing time consists of job setup time and unit production time multiplied by lot size.
5. Group setup time and job setup time are both independent of the sequence of processing.

Let $J_{i\xi}$ ($i = 1, 2, \ldots, N$, $\xi = 1, 2, \ldots, n_i$) denote the ξth job in group G_i ($i = 1, 2, \ldots, N$). When $J_{i\xi}$ is processed in a lot of size $l_{i\xi}$ on machine M_k ($k = 1, 2, \ldots, K$), the job processing time, $p_{i\xi}^k$ of $J_{i\xi}$ on M_k is:

$$p_{i\xi}^k = s_{i\xi}^k + l_{i\xi} u_{i\xi}^k \quad \left(\begin{matrix} i = 1, 2, \ldots, N, \xi = 1, 2, \ldots, n_i \\ k = 1, 2, \ldots, K \end{matrix} \right) \quad (5.7)$$

where $s_{i\xi}^k$ and $u_{i\xi}^k$ are the job setup time and the unit production time on M_k for $J_{i\xi}$, respectively.

Since the job processing time of $J_{i\xi}$ is given by equation 5.7, suppose that the group setup time on M_k for G_i is S_i, the group processing time on M_k for G_i is:

$$Q_i^k = S_i^k + P_i^k, \quad P_i^k = \sum_{\xi=1}^{n_i} p_{i\xi}^k \ (i = 1, 2, \ldots, N) \quad (5.8)$$

where P_i^k is the total processing time on M_k for G_k.

The time available for each of the given machines is supposed to be d_k ($k = 1, 2, \ldots, K$). The problem is to make the optimal selection of groups and jobs to be processed within a given limited time d_k of each machine. As a policy for optimal machine loading, the maximization of production rate, such as, the total amount of parts to be produced, is employed.

Introducing 0-1 type variables, $x_{i\xi}$ ($i = 1, 2 \ldots, N$, $\xi = 1, 2, \ldots, n_i$), that is, $x_{i\xi} = 1$ when $J_{i\xi}$ is selected to produce, and $x_{i\xi} = 0$ when the job is rejected and not produced, the following constraint must be satisfied, since the given time on M_k is d_k.

$$\sum_{i=1}^{N} \left(\sum_{\xi=1}^{n_i} p_{i\xi}^k x_{i\xi} + S_i^k X_i \right) \le d_k \ (k = 1, 2, \ldots, K) \qquad (5.9)$$

where

$$X_i = \begin{cases} 0, \text{if } \sum_{\xi=1}^{n_i} x_{i\xi} = 0 \\ \\ 1, \text{if } \sum_{\xi=1}^{n_i} x_{i\xi} \ge 1 \end{cases} \qquad (5.10)$$

Using the 0-1 type variables, the objective function, which is to maximize the production rate, is to:

Maximize

$$z = \sum_{i=1}^{N} \sum_{\xi=1}^{n_i} w_{i\xi} x_{i\xi} \qquad (5.11)$$

where $w_{i\xi}$ is the size of production lot for $J_{i\xi}$ to be accepted and $1 \le w_{i\xi} \le l_{i\xi}$ ($i = 1, 2, \ldots, N$, $\xi = 1, 2, \ldots, n_i$).

The machine loading problem for group technology applications is now formulated so as to maximize equation 5.11 subject to equation 5.9.

5.3.2 Group Machine Loading Model on a Single Machine

Let us consider a group machine loading problem where a single machine is available for processing jobs [5]. This loading problem is described by:

Maximize

$$z = \sum_{i=1}^{N} \sum_{\xi=1}^{n_i} w_{i\xi} x_{i\xi} \qquad (5.12)$$

subject to

$$\sum_{i=1}^{N} \left(\sum_{\xi=1}^{n_i} p_{i\xi} x_{i\xi} + S_i X_i \right) \le d \qquad (5.13)$$

where

$$X_i = \begin{cases} 0, \text{ if } \displaystyle\sum_{\xi=1}^{n_i} x_{i\xi} = 0 \\[2em] 1, \text{ if } \displaystyle\sum_{\xi=1}^{n_i} x_{i\xi} \ge 1 \end{cases}$$

In an attempt to solve the above problem, the following two cases are considered:

Case 1: If $Q \le d$, where

$$Q = \sum_{i=1}^{N} Q_i = \sum_{i=1}^{N} \left(S_i + \sum_{\xi=1}^{n_i} p_{i\xi} \right), \qquad (5.14)$$

then all the parts under consideration can be accepted, and the optimal solution is:

$$x_{i\xi}^* = 1 \ (i = 1, 2, \ldots, N, \ \xi = 1, 2, \ldots, n_i)$$

$$z^* = z_{\max}$$

where $z_{\max}$ is the maximum of z, that is,

$$z_{\max} = \sum_{i=1}^{N} \sum_{\xi=1}^{n_i} l_{i\xi}$$

Case 2: If $Q > d$, then some parts cannot be accepted, hence, $z^* < z_{\max}$. In order to solve this problem, the branch-and-bound method is employed.

The branch-and-bound method was first developed for solving the traveling salesman problem [6]. This method is basically an implicit enumeration algorithm for iteratively finding an optimal solution to combinatorial problems and is particularly suited to well-structured problems with integer constraints on the variables. Like dynamic programming, it does not deal with a specific mathematical framework, nor does it follow the conventional iterative idea of an optimization process. Its aim is to conduct a reduced search over all possible solutions, the reduction being dependent on how well the problem structure can be exploited.

As its name implies, the branch-and-bound method consists of two fundamental procedures: branching and bounding procedures. Branching is the process of partitioning a large problem into two or more subproblems by a specified rule, and bounding is the process of calculating a lower bound (in the case of minimization) or upper bound (in the case of maximization) for the solution to each subproblem generated in the branching procedure. After each partitioning, for example, in the case of minimization, those sub-problems with bounds that exceed the performance measure of a known feasible solution are excluded from further partitioning. The partitioning is generally repeated until a feasible solution is found such that its performance measure is no longer greater than the bound for any subproblem. When the lower and upper bounds are estimated, the partitioning terminates at a subproblem in which both bounds are equal.

As the branching procedure for the machine loading problem is considered, a node with the maximum upper bound is partitioned such that a new job $J_{i\xi}$ in group G_i with the minimum of $[S_i(1 - X_i) + s_{i\xi}]/l_{i\xi} + u_{i\xi}$ for the remaining jobs (not yet chosen as candidates) is adopted or rejected as a candidate. The size of production lot for the that job, $w_{i\xi}$, is increased up to $l_{i\xi}$ as long as the total production time does not reach the allowable time d.

The bounding procedure for this problem is to calculate the lower bound and upper bound for each node generated in the above branching procedure. The upper bound is estimated as the sum of the current lower bound and $\delta/\{[S_i(1 - X_i) + s_{i\xi}]/l_{i\xi} + u_{i\xi}\}$, where δ is the remaining time available. When $J_{i\xi}$ is adopted, the lower bound at that node is increased by $w_{i\xi}$.

The solution procedure, or termination rule, is that the lower bound and the upper bound are equal at a selected node.

Based on the analytical results mentioned above, the following computational algorithm is developed.

Step 1. Calculate $p_{i\xi}$ by equation 5.7, then Q_i by equation 5.8, and finally Q by equation 5.14. If $Q \leq d$, go to step 2. Otherwise, go to step 3.

Step 2. The optimal solution is

$$x_{i\xi}^* = 1 \ (i = 1, 2, \ldots, N, \ \xi = 1, 2, \ldots, n_i)$$

$$z^* = z_{max} = \sum_{i=1}^{N} \sum_{\xi=1}^{n_i} l_{i\xi}$$

Stop.

Step 3. Generate the initial list: $k = 0$, $K = \{k\}$, $R = \{i\xi/i = 1, 2, \ldots, N$, $\xi = 1, 2, \ldots, n_i\}$, $S = \phi$, $D = 0$, $\delta = d$, $X_i = 0$ $(i = 1, 2, \ldots, N)$, $\underline{z} = 0$, and $\bar{z} = \lceil \delta/\min_{i\xi \in R}\{(S_i + s_{i\xi})/l_{i\xi} + u_{i\xi}\} \rceil.$[†] Go to step 4.

Step 4. Find $\max_{k \in K} \bar{z}$ and denote such index by $\hat{k}$. For the list $\hat{k}$, if $\underline{z} = \bar{z}$, go to step 9. Otherwise, go to step 5.

Step 5. Find $\min_{i\xi \in R}[\{S_i(1 - X_i) + s_{i\xi}\}/l_{i\xi} + u_{i\xi}]$, and denote such index by $\widehat{i\xi}$. Calculate $\hat{D} = D + S_i(1 - X_i) + s_{\widehat{i\xi}} + w_{\widehat{i\xi}}u_{\widehat{i\xi}}$, where $1 \le w_{\widehat{i\xi}} \le l_{\widehat{i\xi}}$. Increase $w_{\widehat{i\xi}}$ up to $l_{\widehat{i\xi}}$ as long as $\hat{D} \le d$; otherwise, replace $l_{\widehat{i\xi}}$ by $w_{\widehat{i\xi}}$ which satisfies the relation: $\hat{D} \le d \le \hat{D} + u_{\widehat{i\xi}}$. If $w_{\widehat{i\xi}} = 0$, go to step 6; if $\hat{D} = d$, go to step 7; and if $\hat{D} < d$, go to step 8.

Step 6. Set $R = R - \{\widehat{i\xi}\}$ for the list $\hat{k}$. If $R = \phi$, set $\underline{z} = \bar{z}$. Return to step 4.

Step 7. Generate a new list: $k = k + 1$, $K = K + \{k\} - \{\hat{k}\}$ $S = S + \{\widehat{i\xi}\}$, $\underline{z} = \underline{z} + w_{\widehat{i\xi}}$, and $\bar{z} = \underline{z}$. Return to step 4.

Step 8. Branch the list $\hat{k}$ and generate two new lists: $k = k + 1$, $K = K + \{k\} - \{\hat{k}\}$, $R = R - \{\widehat{i\xi}\}$, $S = S$, $D = D$, $\delta = \delta$, $\underline{z} = \underline{z}$, and $\bar{z} = \underline{z} + \lceil \delta/\min_{i\xi \in R}[\{S_i(1 - X_i) + s_{i\xi}\}/l_{i\xi} + u_{i\xi}] \rceil$ for $R \ne \phi$ or $\bar{z} = \underline{z}$ for $R = \phi$; and $k = k + 1$, $K = K + \{k\}$, $R = R$, $S = S + \{\widehat{i\xi}\}$, $D = \hat{D}$, $\delta = d - D$, $X_i = 1$,

---

[†] $\lceil A \rceil$ is a Gaussian notation, implying a greatest integer value equal to or less than A.

Table 5.4. Basic data for a single-machine group loading [5]

Group	Part	Lot Size	Group Setup Time	Job Setup Time	Unit Production Time
i	j	l_{ij}	S_i	s_{ij}	P_{ij}
Number	Number	pcs	min	min/lot	min/pc
1	1	30	40	19	6
	2	10		8	2
2	1	20		10	17
	2	50	35	9	9
	3	30		15	7
3	1	20	20	5	12
	2	60		13	6
4	1	20		6	16
	2	10	45	10	13
	3	40		20	15

Note: Allowable time $D = 40$ (hr).

Table 5.5. Optimal solutions for a single-machine group loading [5]

Group Number		1			2			3			4	
Part Number		1	2	3	1	2	3	1	2	3	2	3
Lot Size Demanded	pcs	30	10	20	50	30	20	20	60	40	10	40
Accept(A) or Reject(R)		A	A	R	A	A	A	R	A	A	A	A
Production Amount	pcs	30	10	—	50	30	20	—	60	40	7	40
Production Time	min/lot	199	28	—	459	225	245	—	373	620	101	620
Group Production Time	min	267			719			638			766	
Total Production Amount	pcs	247										

Total Production Time: 2390 min Remaining Time: 10 min

$\underline{z} = \underline{z} + w_{i\xi}$ and $\overline{z} = \underline{z} + [\delta/\min_{i\xi\epsilon R}[\{S_i(1 - X_i) + s_{i\xi}\}/l_{i\xi} + u_{i\xi}]]$ for $R \neq \phi$
or $\overline{z} = z$ for $R = \phi$. Return to step 4.

Step 9. The optimal solution is obtained in the list $\hat{k}$: by setting
$S^* = S$,

$$x_{i\xi}^* = 1 \text{ for all } i\xi\epsilon S^*$$

$$x_{i\xi}^* = 0 \text{ otherwise}$$

$$z^* = \overline{z}$$

Stop.

Example 5.3. Using the computational algorithm developed in the previous section, a numerical example for determining the optimal parts to be produced is presented. Data for the example are given as shown in table 5.4. The optimal parts to be produced for production in a limited capacity of the production facility (40 hours) are obtained by the optimizing algorithm in the previous section, and indicated by "A" in table 5.5.

References

1. Joshi, V.M. *Management Science—A survey of Quantitative Decision-Making Techniques.* North Scituate, Massachusetts: Duxbury Press, pp. 359–363, 1980.
2. Ross, G.T., and Soland, R.M. "A Branch-and-Bound Algorithm for the Generalized Assignment Problem." *Mathematical Programming*, 8, pp. 91–103, 1975.
3. Balas, E. "An Additive Algorithm for Solving Linear Program with Zero-One Variables." *Operations Research*, 8(1), pp. 517–546, 1965.
4. Hitomi, K. *Production Management Engineering.* (Japanese) Tokyo: Corona Publishing Co., pp. 46–47, 1978.
5. Hitomi, K., and Ham, I. "Machine Loading for Group Technology Applications." *CIRP Annals*, 26 (August 1977), pp. 279–281.
6. Little, J.D.C., Murty, K.G., Sweeny, D.W., and Karel, C. "An Algorithm for the Traveling Salesman Problem." *Operations Research*, 11(6), pp. 972–989, 1963.

6 GROUP MACHINE LOADING WITH VARIABLE PROCESSING TIMES

6.1 Basic Models of Production Systems with Variable Processing Times

In most cases in the field of production planning and scheduling, the processing time required to complete a specified operation of a job is set as a constant. In the previous chapter, the machine loading models were constructed under the assumption that the processing time is a constant. In practical situations, however, it is possible to vary the processing times by actively changing manufacturing conditions, especially machining speeds. In these cases, some modifications must be made to the production planning and scheduling models. In order to solve those models, a new type of analysis must be made allowing for variation in processing times and costs. This chapter treats the machine loading models with variable processing times. First, a basic production model with variable processing times is covered, and then it is extended to the machine loading models.

A basic model of production systems with variable processing times is as follows [1]:

1. Unit production time. This is the time needed to manufacture a unit piece of a product. This unit production time u(min/pc), is assumed to be composed of the preparation time (or setup time), machining time, and tool-replacement time, and is expressed as a function of machining speed, v(m/min), as follows:

$$u = a + t + b\frac{t}{T}$$

$$= a + \frac{\lambda}{v} + \frac{\lambda b}{C^{\frac{1}{n}}} v^{\frac{1}{n}-1} \tag{6.1}$$

where a is the preparation time (min/pc), t is actual machining time, b is tool replacement time (min/edge), T is the tool life (min/edge), λ is the machining constant, and n and C are parameters for the Taylor tool-life equation.

The time curve with regard to machining speed given by equation 6.1 has a minimal point $v^{(t)}$, which is called the "maximum-production-rate or minimum-production-time machining speed," and is determined by setting the derivative of equation 6.1 to v equals zero:

$$v^{(t)} = C\bigg/\left[\left(\frac{1}{n} - 1\right)b \right]^{n} \tag{6.2}$$

2. Unit production cost. This is the cost required to manufacture a unit piece of product. This cost, q($/pc), consists of the preparation cost, machining cost, and tool-replacement cost, and is expressed as a function of machining speed as follows:

$$q = \alpha a + (\alpha + \beta)t + (\alpha b + \gamma)\frac{t}{T}$$

$$= \alpha a + (\alpha + \beta)\frac{\lambda}{v} + (\alpha b + \gamma)\frac{\lambda}{C^{\frac{1}{n}}} v^{\frac{1}{n}-1} \tag{6.3}$$

where α is the direct labor cost and overhead ($/min), β is the machining overhead ($/min), and γ is the tool cost ($/edge).

The cost curve with regard to machining speed given by equation 6.3 has a minimal point $v^{(c)}$, which is called the "minimum-production-cost machining speed" and is also determined by setting the derivative of equation 6.3 to v equals zero:

$$v^{(c)} = C\left[\left(\frac{n}{1-n}\right)\left(\frac{\alpha + \beta}{\alpha b + \gamma}\right) \right]^{n} \tag{6.4}$$

3. Unit profit. This is the gain obtained by producing a unit piece of product. This profit is the unit revenue or selling price minus unit production cost:

$$g = e - q \qquad (6.5)$$

where e is the unit revenue (\$/pc).

The profit rate, which in this book is defined as the profit in a given time period, is expressed:

$$f = \frac{g}{u} = \frac{e - \left[\alpha a + (\alpha + \beta)\dfrac{\lambda}{v} + (\alpha b + \gamma)\dfrac{\lambda}{C^{\frac{1}{n}}} v^{\frac{1}{n}-1} \right]}{a + \dfrac{\lambda}{v} + \dfrac{b\lambda}{C^{\frac{1}{n}}} v^{\frac{1}{n}-1}} \qquad (6.6)$$

A maximal point, $v^{(p)}$, which is called the "maximum-profit-rate machining speed," for the machining speed curve is determined by differentiating equation 6.6 with respect to machining speed and setting it to equal zero. However, this optimal speed is not explicitly expressed like equation 6.2 or 6.4. It is calculated by the following general equation:

$$(1 - n)(\gamma a + eb)v^{\frac{1}{n}} + \lambda(\gamma - \beta b)v^{\frac{1}{n}-1} - nC^{\frac{1}{n}}(e + \beta a) = 0 \qquad (6.7)$$

Between the maximum-production-rate machining speed, $v^{(t)}$, the minimum-cost machining speed, $v^{(c)}$, and the maximum-profit-rate machining speed, $v^{(p)}$, a reasonable assumption of $v^{(c)} < v^{(t)}$ [2] can be made; then there exists the following noteworthy relationship:

$$v^{(c)} < v^{(p)} < v^{(t)} \qquad (6.8)$$

A speed range between the minimum-cost machining speed and the maximum-production-rate machining speed is called the "high-efficiency speed range," which means that any machining speed in this range is preferable from the managerial standpoint. A speed in this range is called "high-efficiency machining speed" and is denoted by $v^{(e)}$.

For the profit-rate function, it follows that $f(v)$ is positive, continuous, and has a unique maximum point $v^{(f)}$ inside the efficiency range $E = [v^{(c)}, v^{(t)}]$.

Example 6.1. Compute optimal machining speeds under three kinds of criteria for production data as given in the following:

Tool-life parameters

slope constant n	0.23
1-min tool life machining speed C (m/min)	430

Machining parameters

    machining constant λ 157

Time parameters

    preparation time a (min/pc)   0.75

    tool-replacement time b (min/edge)   1.50

Cost parameters

    direct labor cost and overhead α ($/min)   0.50

    machining overhead cost β ($/min)   0.05

    tool cost γ ($/edge)   2.5

    gross revenue g ($/pc)   32

Based upon the above data, three kinds of optimal machining speeds are calculated by equations 6.2, 6.4, and 6.7, and we obtain:

the minimum-cost machining speed (m/min) $v^{(c)} = 216$

the maximum-profit-rate machining speed (m/min) $v^{(p)} = 278$

the maximum-production-rate machining speed (m/min) $v^{(t)} = 297$

6.2 Basic Machine Loading Model with Variable Processing Times

6.2.1 Basic Model

In the previous chapter, a basic machine loading model was formulated as the problem of determining product items, so as to maximize the production amount subject to the available-time constraints. In the model the processing times were set constant. In this section, however, a more general machine loading problem with variable processing times and costs is treated as follows [3]:

    n product items (or jobs) are to be processed on a single-stage production system with a limited time d. It is assumed that the processing time for a job is variable depending on the machining speed and given by equation 6.1. After determining the optimal kinds of jobs to be produced, there still exist decision variables: that is, machining speeds. Thus the machine loading problem with variable processing times to be solved will determine the optimal kinds of jobs to be produced within a limited time available as well as decide the optimal machining speeds for all the jobs to be accepted. This will maximize a first measure of performance such as the production amount of product items and then minimize a second measure of performance such as the total production cost.

A machine loading model with variable processing times is defined as follows:

Introducing a 0-1 type variable x_i ($i = 1, 2, \ldots, n$); that is, $x_i = 1$ when the product item J_i is selected to be produced, and $x_i = 0$ when the product item J_i is rejected, the following constraint must be satisfied:

$$\sum_{i=1}^{n} u_i x_i \leq d \qquad (6.9)$$

where u_i is the production time of J_i and is given by equation 6.1, and d is the limited time available.

Let us denote by U the set $\{1, 2, \ldots, n\}$ of all product items. The rejection and acceptance sets are $R = \{i/x_i = 0, i \in U\}$ and $S = \{i/x_i = 1, i \in U\}$, respectively. The remaining set is then: $V = U - (R + S)$

Then the total time expended is:

$$D = \sum_{i \in S} u_i(v_i) \qquad (6.10)$$

Hence, the time slack is:

$$\delta = d - D = d - \sum_{i \in S} u_i(v_i) \qquad (6.11)$$

As a criterion for optimally determining kinds of product items, the social objective is employed; that is, the maximization of the total number of product items to be produced. Then the objective function is given by:

$$z = \sum_{i=1}^{n} x_i \qquad (6.12)$$

The machine loading problem with variable processing times is now formulated to maximize equation 6.12 subject to equation 6.9.

6.2.2 Analysis of Machine Loading Model with Variable Processing Times

In an attempt to solve the above problem, the following three cases are considered.

Case 1: The maximum of z is increased to n by decreasing $u_i(v_i)$, which is the variable coefficient of the constraint. Since $u_i(v_i)$ has a minimal point $v_i^{(t)}$, the following proposition holds.

Proposition 1. If $\Sigma_{i=1}^{n} u_i(v_i^{(t)}) = d$, then the optimal solution is:

$$x_i^* = 1, \qquad v_i^* = v_i^{(t)} \qquad (i = 1, 2, \ldots, n)$$

$$z^* = n, \qquad \delta^* = 0 \qquad\qquad\qquad\qquad\qquad (6.13)$$

In this case all the product items are accepted.

Case 2: If $\Sigma_{i=1}^{n} u_i(v_i^{(t)}) > d$, the problem is replaced by the following ordinary 0-1 type linear program.

(0-1 LP) maximize equation 6.12 subject to

$$\sum_{i=1}^{n} u_i^{(t)} x_i \le d$$

$$x_i = 0 \text{ or } 1 \ (i = 1, 2, \ldots, n) \qquad\qquad (6.14)$$

where $u_i^{(t)}$ is the minimum production time (constant). It is given by

$$u_i^{(t)} = u_i(v_i^{(t)})$$

$$= a_i + \frac{\lambda_i}{(1 - n_i)C_i} \left[\left(\frac{1}{n_i} - 1 \right) b_i \right]^{n_i} \qquad (6.15)$$

In this case, all product items cannot be accepted even if the minimum-time speeds are employed in producing them; the total production time needed exceeds the allowable limit.

The above 0-1 LP can easily be solved by the branch-and-bound algorithm which is shown in the algorithm in the next section (steps 4 through 10).

Case 3: If $\Sigma_{i=1}^{n} u_i(v_i^{(t)}) < d$, it is certainly possible that all product items can be accepted: $R^* = \phi$ and $S^* = U$, hence,

$$x_i^* = 1 \text{ for all } i \in S^*, z^* = n \qquad\qquad (6.16)$$

In this case the following time slack occurs:

$$\delta = d - \sum_{i \in S^*} u_i(v_i^{(t)}) \qquad\qquad\qquad (6.17)$$

Speed variables v_i for $i \in S^*$ can take any feasible values as long as the constraint is satisfied. To determine unique feasible speed values for all $i \in S^*$, let us try to maximize the total profit obtained by utilizing the time slack. The following nonlinear program is to be solved instead of solving the original problem.

(NP) Maximize

$$w = \sum_{i \in S*} g_i(v_i) \tag{6.18}$$

subject to

$$\sum_{i \in S*} u_i(v_i) \leq d \tag{6.19}$$

The optimal solution v_i^* to this NP must satisfy the Kuhn-Tucker's necessary condition [4]. Hence, for a nonnegative constant λ^*,

$$\sum_{i \in S*} dg(v_i^*)/dv_i - \lambda^* \sum_{i \in S*} du_i(v_i^*)/dv_i = 0 \tag{6.20}$$

$$\lambda^* \left\{ d - \sum_{i \in S*} u_i(v_i^*) \right\} = \lambda^* \delta^* = 0 \tag{6.21}$$

and

$$\sum_{i \in S*} u_i(v_i^*) \leq d, \ \delta^* = d - \sum_{i \in S*} u_i(v_i^*) \geq 0 \tag{6.22}$$

The function, called "efficiency-sensitivity function," is defined as

$$r_i(v_i) = \frac{dg_i(v_i)}{du_i(v_i)}$$

$$= \frac{\dfrac{\beta_i}{v_i^2} - \left(\dfrac{1}{n_i} - 1 \right) \gamma_i v_i^{\frac{1}{n_i}-2} / C_i^{\frac{1}{n_i}}}{-\dfrac{1}{v_i^2} + \left(\dfrac{1}{n_i} - 1 \right) b_i v_i^{\frac{1}{n_i}-2} / C_i^{\frac{1}{n_i}}} - \alpha \tag{6.23}$$

This function is nonnegative, monotone increasing from 0 to ∞ on $E_i = [v_i^{(g)}, v_i^{(t)}]$ where $v_i^{(g)}$ and $v_i^{(t)}$ are the maximal and the minimal points of the profit and the time functions, $g_i(v_i)$ and $u_i(v_i)$, respectively: that is, $v_i^{(t)}$ is given by equation 6.2 and $v_i^{(g)}$ by equation 6.4, since $dg/dv = -dq/dv = 0$. Consequently, there exists the inverse function of $r_i(v_i)$ for $\lambda > 0$ which is denoted by $r_i^{-1}(\lambda) \in E_i$.

From the above discussion the following proposition results.

Proposition 2. For the optimal solution to NP, the following must be satisfied:

1. $\lambda^* > 0$ implies $\delta^* = 0$ and $v_i^* = r_i^{-1}(\lambda^*) \in (v_i^{(g)}, v_i^{(t)})$ for all $i \in S*$.
2. $\lambda^* = 0$ implies $\delta^* \geq 0$ and $v_i^* = v_i^{(g)}$ for all $i \in S*$.

6.2.3 Optimizing Algorithm

Based on the analytical results mentioned above, the following computational algorithm is presented for solving the problem:

Step 1. Obtain $v_i^{(t)}$ for all $i \in U$ and calculate $u_i(v_i^{(t)})$ for all $i \in U$ and $D = \Sigma_{i \in U} u_i(v_i^{(t)})$. If $D = d$, go to step 2; if $D < d$, go to step 3; and if $D > d$, go to step 4.

Step 2. Set $S^* = U$. The optimal solution is:

$$x_i^* = 1, \qquad v_i^* = v_i^{(t)} \text{ for all } i \in S^*$$

$$z^* = n, \qquad \delta^* = 0$$

Stop.

Step 3. Set $S^* = U$ and $\lambda > 0$. Calculate $v_{i_0} = r_i^{-1}(\lambda) \in E_i$ for all $i \in S^*$, and ascertain $\Sigma_{i \in S^*} u(v_{i_0}) = d$. The optimal solution is:

$$x_i^* = 1, \qquad v_i^* = v_{i_0} \text{ for all } i \in S^*$$

$$z^* = n, \qquad \delta^* = 0$$

Stop.

Step 4. Set $u_i^{(t)} = u_i(v_i^{(t)})$ for all $i \in U$ and generate the initial list: $k = 0$, $K = \{k\}$, $R = U$, $S = \phi$, $D = 0$, $\delta = d$, $\underline{z} = 0$, and $\bar{z} = \lceil \delta/\min_{i \in R} u_i^{(t)} \rceil$. Go to step 5.

Step 5. Find $\max_{k \in K} \bar{z}$ and denote such index by $\hat{k}$. For the list $\hat{k}$, if $\underline{z} = \bar{z}$, go to step 10; otherwise, go to step 6.

Step 6. Find $\tau = \min_{i \in R} u_i^{(t)}$ and denote such index by $\hat{i}$. Calculate $\hat{D} = D + \tau$. If $\hat{D} > d$, go to step 7; if $\hat{D} = d$, go to step 8; and if $\hat{D} < d$, go to step 9.

Step 7. Set $R = R - \{\hat{i}\}$ for the list and return to step 6.

Step 8. Generate a new list: $k = k + 1$, $K = K + \{k\} - \{\hat{k}\}$, $S = S + \{\hat{i}\}$, $\delta = 0$ and $\underline{z} = \underline{z} + 1 = \bar{z}$. Return to step 5.

Step 9. Branch the list $\hat{k}$ and generate two new lists: $k = k + 1$, $K = K + \{k\} - \{\hat{k}\}$, $R = R - \{\hat{i}\}$, $S = S$, $D = D$, $\delta = \delta$, $\underline{z} = \underline{z}$, and $\bar{z} = \underline{z} + \lceil \delta/\min_{i \in R} u_i^{(t)} \rceil$ for $R \neq \phi$ or $\bar{z} = \underline{z}$ for $R = \phi$; and $k = k + 1$, $K = K + \{k\}$, $R = R$, $S = S + \{\hat{i}\}$, $D = \hat{D}$, $\delta = d - D$, $\underline{z} = \underline{z} + 1$, and $\bar{z} = \underline{z} + \lceil \delta/\min_{i \in R} u_i^{(t)} \rceil$ for $S \neq \phi$ or $\bar{z} = \underline{z}$ for $R = \phi$. Return to step 5.

Step 10. The optimal solution is obtained in the list $\hat{k}$: By setting $S^* = S$,

$$x_i^* = 1, \qquad v_i^* = v_i^{(t)} \text{ for all } i \in S^*$$

$$x_i^* = 0, \qquad v_i^* = \text{indefinite for all } i \in U - S^*$$

$$z^* = \bar{z}, \qquad \delta^* = \delta$$

Stop.

Example 6.2. When production information as shown in table 6.1—particularly product items (column 1) and order amounts (column 2)—are given, an optimal plan for the maximization of the total amount of product items to produce is obtained. This is indicated in table 6.2 and found by using the optimizing algorithm developed above. In this case, the production time and cost for product i ($i = 1, 2, \ldots, n$) of order amount m_i are:

$$u_i = s_i + m_i \left(a_i + \frac{\lambda_i}{v_i} + \frac{\lambda_i b_i}{C_i^{\frac{1}{n_i}}} v_i^{\frac{1}{n_i} - 1} \right) \tag{6.24}$$

$$q_i = c_i + (\alpha + \beta_i)s_i + m_i \left[h_i + \alpha a_i + (\alpha + \beta_i)\frac{\lambda_i}{v_i} \right.$$

$$\left. + (\alpha b_i + \gamma_i) \frac{\lambda_i}{C_i^{\frac{1}{n_i}}} v_i^{\frac{1}{n_i} - 1} \right] \tag{6.25}$$

Table 6.1(a).   Production information for machine loading problem [3]

Product Item	Order Amount	Material Parameter		Machining Parameter		Tool Life Parameter	
		Work Diameter	Length	Depth of Cut*	Feed Rate	Slope Constant	1 min Tool Life Speed
i	m_i	D_i	L_i	d_i	f_i	n_i	C_i
Number	pcs	mm	mm	mm	mm/rev		mm/min
1	80	50	150	1.00	0.30	0.25	500.0
2	100	100	200	2.00	0.15	0.20	450.0
3	120	100	200	1.50	0.10	0.33	600.0
4	70	75	200	1.00	0.20	0.33	550.0
5	80	75	200	1.50	0.25	0.20	600.0
6	60	150	250	2.00	0.10	0.20	500.0
7	150	30	100	2.00	0.20	0.25	400.0
8	70	200	400	2.50	0.10	0.25	700.0
9	90	150	400	1.50	0.25	0.33	650.0
10	80	150	300	1.00	0.05	0.25	600.0

*This is not used in computation.

Table 6.1(b). Production information for machine loading problem [3]

	Time Parameter			Cost Parameter					
Product Item	Setup Time	Preparation Time	Tool Exchange Time	Setup Cost	Machining Overhead Cost	Tool Cost	Direct Labor Cost & Overhead	Material Cost	Unit Revenue
i	s_i	a_i	b_i	c_i	β_i	γ	α	h_i	e_i
Number	min/lot	min/pc	min/edge	$/lot	$/min	$/edge	$/min	$/pc	$/pc
1	15.00	1.00	0.75	195	2	100	13	50	200
2	10.00	2.00	1.00	130	3	150	13	20	120
3	20.00	0.75	1.50	260	3	200	13	70	220
4	20.00	1.50	2.00	260	4	200	13	30	130
5	15.00	1.50	1.00	195	4	150	13	10	60
6	30.00	3.00	2.00	390	6	300	13	80	380
7	5.00	0.75	0.50	65	1	75	13	15	65
8	40.00	5.00	2.00	520	10	500	13	150	700
9	45.00	4.00	3.00	585	8	400	13	90	440
10	30.00	2.00	1.50	390	5	350	13	200	850

Allowable Production Time	d	min	2400

Table 6.2. Maximization of the total amount of product items in machine loading problem [3]

Optimal Product Mix Based on Order Amount Maximization

Order Entry

	Total	1	2	3	4	5	6	7	8	9	10
Order Number		1	2	3	4	5	6	7	8	9	10
Product Number		1	2	3	4	5	6	7	8	9	10
Order Amount (pcs)		80	100	120	70	80	60	150	70	90	80
Optimal Solution											
Decision (Accept or Reject)		Accept	Accept	Accept	Accept	Accept	Accept	Accept	Reject	Accept	Reject
Optimal Cutting Speed (m/min)		408	341	415	348	454	329	381	–	358	–
Tool Life (min/edge)		2.25	4.00	3.05	4.06	4.00	8.00	1.50	–	6.09	–
Production Amount (pcs)		80	100	120	70	80	60	150	–	66	–
Production Time (min/lot)		115.52	363.55	380.86	196.07	204.09	477.85	143.58	–	516.43	–
Total Production Amount (pcs)	726										
Total Production Time (min)	2397.93										
Total Time Slack (min)	2.07										
Total Profit ($)	24317										

where s_i and c_i are the setup time and cost, respectively, per lot for product i, and h_i is the material cost for product i. The machining constant is computed by

$$\lambda_i = \frac{\pi D_i L_i}{1000 f_i} \qquad (6.26)$$

where D_i and L_i are work diameter and work length of product i, and f_i is feed rate in machining product i. (These data are indicated in table 6.1)

When selecting the optimizing criterion for product items to be produced, the total profit (given by equation 6.18) can be considered.

The machine loading problem with variable processing times can also be solved under the criterion of maximizing the total profit and by the solution procedure similar to the one for the maximum total amount.

6.3 Group Machine Loading Model with Variable Processing Times: A Single-Stage Case

6.3.1 Basic Single-Stage Group Machine Loading Model with Variable Processing Times

In the previous section, a basic machine loading model with variable processing times was constructed. In this section, let us consider a single-stage group machine loading model with variable processing times, which is associated with the concept of group technology [5].

In addition to the fundamental assumptions of the group machine loading model mentioned in the previous chapter, it is assumed that the unit production time and cost for product item (part) are variable depending on machining speed. Although several kinds of criteria are considered for optimally determining product items to be produced, we employ as an optimizing criterion the maximization of the production rate; that is, the total amount of product items to produce in a limited time available.

The unit production time $u_{i\xi}$, (min/pc), of part ($J_{i\xi}$) which belongs to group i (G_i) is expressed as a function of machining speed, $v_{i\xi}$ (m/min) for the part as follows:

$$u_{i\xi} = a_{i\xi} + \frac{\lambda_{i\xi}}{v_{i\xi}} + \frac{\lambda_{i\xi} b_{i\xi}}{C_{i\xi}^{\frac{1}{n_{i\xi}}}} v_{i\xi}^{\frac{1}{n_{i\xi}}-1} \qquad (6.27)$$

$$(i = 1, 2, \ldots, N, \xi = 1, 2, \ldots, n_i)$$

where $a_{i\xi}$ is preparation time (min/pc), $b_{i\xi}$ is tool replacement time (min/edge), $T_{i\xi}$ is tool life (min/edge), $\lambda_{i\xi}$ is a machining constant, $n_{i\xi}$ and $C_{i\xi}$ are parameters for the Taylor tool-life equation, and $v_{i\xi}$ is the machining speed (decision variable) for $J_{i\xi}$.

Then the maximum production-rate machining speed for $J_{i\xi}$ is given by:

$$v_{i\xi}^{(t)} = \frac{C_{i\xi}}{\left[\left(\dfrac{1}{n_{i\xi}} - 1 \right) b_{i\xi} \right]^{n_{i\xi}}}$$

$$(i = 1, 2, \ldots, N, \; \xi = 1, 2, \ldots, n_i) \qquad (6.28)$$

When processing $J_{i\xi}$ in a lot size $l_{i\xi}$, the job processing time of $J_{i\xi}$ is:

$$p_{i\xi} = s_{i\xi} + l_{i\xi} u_{i\xi}(v_{i\xi}) \; (i = 1, 2, \ldots, N, \; \xi = 1, 2, \ldots, n_i) (6.29)$$

where $s_{i\xi}$ is the job setup time (min/lot) for $J_{i\xi}$.

Since the job processing time of $J_{i\xi}$ is given by equation 6.29, which supposes that the group setup time for G_i is S_i(min), the group processing time for G_i is:

$$Q_i = S_i + P_i, \; P_i = \sum_{\xi=1}^{n_i} p_{i\xi} \qquad (6.30)$$

$$(i = 1, 2, \ldots, N)$$

Unit production cost, $q_{i\xi}$($/pc) of $J_{i\xi}$ is expressed as a function of machining speed $v_{i\xi}$ (m/min) as follows:

$$q_{i\xi} = \alpha a_{i\xi} + (\alpha + \beta_{i\xi}) \frac{\lambda_{i\xi}}{v_{i\xi}}$$

$$+ (\alpha b_{i\xi} + \gamma_{i\xi}) \frac{\lambda_{i\xi}}{C_{i\xi}^{\frac{1}{n_{i\xi}}}} v_{i\xi}^{\frac{1}{n_{i\xi}}-1}$$

$$(i = 1, 2, \ldots, N, \; \xi = 1, 2, \ldots, n_i) \qquad (6.31)$$

where α is direct labor cost and overhead ($/min), $\beta_{i\xi}$ is machining overhead ($/min), and $\gamma_{i\xi}$ is tool cost ($/edge) for $J_{i\xi}$. Then the minimum-production-cost machining speed is given by:

$$v_{i\xi}^{(c)} = C_{i\xi} \left[\left(\frac{n_{i\xi}}{1 - n_{i\xi}} \right) \left(\frac{\alpha + \beta_{i\xi}}{\alpha b_{i\xi} + \gamma_{i\xi}} \right) \right]^{n_{i\xi}}$$

$$(i = 1, 2, \ldots, N, \; \xi = 1, 2, \ldots, n_i) \qquad (6.32)$$

Introducing the same 0-1 type variables, $x_{i\xi}$ ($i = 1, 2, \ldots, N, \xi = 1, 2, \ldots, n_i$) as in the previous section, the following constraint must be satisfied:

$$\sum_{i=1}^{N} \left(\sum_{\xi=1}^{n_i} p_{i\xi} x_{i\xi} + S_i X_i \right) \leq d \qquad (6.33)$$

where

$$X_i = \begin{cases} 0, \text{ if } \sum\limits_{\xi=1}^{n_i} x_{i\xi} = 0 \\[2em] 1, \text{ if } \sum\limits_{\xi=1}^{n_i} x_{i\xi} \geq 1 \end{cases} \qquad (6.34)$$

and d is the limited time available.

The policy to be employed for optimal machine loading is to maximize the total amount of parts to produce in a limited time available, d. Hence, the objective function is to:

Maximize

$$z = \sum_{i=1}^{N} \sum_{\xi=1}^{n_i} l_{i\xi} x_{i\xi} \qquad (6.35)$$

The machine loading problem for group technology is now formulated so as to maximize equation 6.35 subject to equation 6.33.

6.3.2 Analysis of Single-Stage Group Machine Loading Model

In an attempt to solve the above problem, the following three cases are considered as in the previous section.

Case 1:   The maximum of z is obtained when all $x_{i\xi}$ are 1; that is

$$z_{\max} = \sum_{i=1}^{N} \sum_{\xi=1}^{n_i} l_{i\xi}$$

If such a case occurs at all minimal points of time curves, then the optimal solution is easily obtained as follows:

Proposition 3. If

$$Q \equiv \sum_{i=1}^{N} Q_i^{(t)} = \sum_{i=1}^{N} \left(S_i + \sum_{\xi=1}^{n_i} p_{i\xi}^{(t)} \right) = d \qquad (6.36)$$

where

$$\left. \begin{aligned} p_{i\xi}^{(t)} &= s_{i\xi} + l_{i\xi} u_{i\xi}^{(t)} \\ u_{i\xi}^{(t)} &= u_{i\xi}(v_{i\xi}^{(t)}) \\ &= a_{i\xi} + \frac{\lambda_{i\xi}}{(1 - n_{i\xi}) C_{i\xi}} \left[\left(\frac{1}{n_{i\xi}} - 1 \right) b_{i\xi} \right]^{n_{i\xi}} \\ (i &= 1, 2, \ldots, N, \xi = 1, 2, \ldots, n_i) \end{aligned} \right\} \qquad (6.37)$$

then the optimal solution is:

$$\left. \begin{aligned} x_{i\xi} &= 1, \quad v_{i\xi}^* = v_{i\xi}^{(t)} \\ z^* &= z_{\max} \end{aligned} \right\} \qquad (6.38)$$

The following notations are defined:

$U =$ set of all parts $= \{i\xi \,|\, i = 1, 2, \ldots, N, \xi = 1, 2, \ldots, n_i\}$

$R =$ rejection set $= \{i\xi \,|\, x_{i\xi} = 0, i\xi \in U\}$

$S =$ acceptance set $= \{i\xi \,|\, x_{i\xi} = 1, i\xi \in U\}$

Then in Case 1, $R^* = \phi$ and $S^* = U$.

Case 2: If $Q > d$, then the problem is replaced by the following 0-1 type linear program, since machining speeds, $v_{i\xi}$ are constants ($= v_{i\xi}^{(t)}$) and there are no more decision variables.

Maximize equation 6.35 subject to equation 6.33, where

$$p_{i\xi} = p_{i\xi}^{(t)} \qquad (6.39)$$

The solution procedure for this program is indicated by steps 4 through 10 in the optimizing algorithm mentioned later. In these steps, the branch-and-bound method is employed by sequentially examining a part with a least unit production time including setup time as the candidate. In Case 2, all product items cannot be accepted, even if the minimum-time speeds are employed in producing them, since the total production time needed exceeds the allowable limit; hence, $R^* \neq \phi$ and $S^* \neq U$ and $z^* < z_{\max}$.

Case 3: If $Q < d$, it is certain that all parts can be accepted: $R^* = \phi$, and $S^* = U$, hence,

$$\left.\begin{array}{l} x_{i\xi}^* = 1 \quad \text{for all } i\xi \in U \\[2ex] z^* = z_{\max} \end{array}\right\} \tag{6.40}$$

In this case, if the minimum-time speeds are employed for all parts, then the following time slack occurs.

$$\delta = d - Q > 0 \tag{6.41}$$

Speed variables $v_{i\xi}$ can take any feasible values as long as the constraint 6.33 is satisfied. To determine unique feasible speed values for machining all parts, let us try to minimize the total cost needed by utilizing the above time slack.

It is reasonable to consider that the unit production time is the smallest at the minimum-production-time-speed, and that this speed is greater than the minimum-production-cost speed. On the other hand, the unit production cost is the least at the minimum-production-cost speed and increases with an increase in machining speed up to the minimum-production-time speed. Therefore, by utilizing the time slack given by equation 6.41, the total cost will be reduced by decreasing the machining speed from the minimum-production-time speed, which is temporarily predetermined optimal speed value, and thus decreasing the unit production cost. Based on this idea, the following nonlinear program is obtained, where decision variables are $v_{i\xi}$ for all i and ξ.

Minimize

$$Y = \sum_{i=1}^{N} \left[\alpha S_i + \sum_{\xi=1}^{n_i} \{\alpha s_{i\xi} + l_{i\xi} q_{i\xi}(v_{i\xi})\} \right] \tag{6.42}$$

subject to

$$\sum_{i=1}^{N} \left[S_i + \sum_{\xi=1}^{n_i} \{s_{i\xi} + l_{i\xi} u_{i\xi}(v_{i\xi})\} \right] \leq d \tag{6.43}$$

This reduces to the following problem by neglecting the constraint which does not play a significant role in solving the current problem.

Minimize

$$Y' = \sum_{i=1}^{N} \sum_{\xi=1}^{n_i} l_{i\xi} q_{i\xi}(v_{i\xi}) \tag{6.44}$$

subject to

$$\sum_{i=1}^{N} \sum_{\xi=1}^{n_i} l_{i\xi} u_{i\xi}(v_{i\xi}) \le d_0 \tag{6.45}$$

$v_{i\xi}$ is continuous and positive for all i and ξ where

$$d_0 = d - \sum_{i=1}^{N} \left(S_i + \sum_{\xi=1}^{n_i} s_{i\xi} \right) = \text{constant} \tag{6.46}$$

The optimal solution $v_{i\xi}^*$ to this nonlinear program must satisfy the Kuhn-Tucker necessary condition. Hence, for a nonnegative constant μ^*,

$$\sum_{i=1}^{N} \sum_{\xi=1}^{n_i} l_{i\xi} \frac{dq_{i\xi}(v_{i\xi}^*)}{dv_{i\xi}} + \mu^* \sum_{i=1}^{N} \sum_{\xi=1}^{n_i} l_{i\xi} \frac{du_{i\xi}(v_{i\xi}^*)}{dv_{i\xi}} = 0 \tag{6.47}$$

$$\mu^* \left\{ d_0 - \sum_{i=1}^{N} \sum_{\xi=1}^{n_i} l_{i\xi} u_{i\xi}(v_{i\xi}^*) \right\} = \mu^* \delta^* = 0 \tag{6.48}$$

and

$$\left. \begin{array}{c} \displaystyle\sum_{i=1}^{N} \sum_{\xi=1}^{n_i} l_{i\xi} u_{i\xi}(v_{i\xi}^*) \le d_0 \\[2em] \delta^* = d_0 - \displaystyle\sum_{i=1}^{N} \sum_{\xi=1}^{n_i} l_{i\xi} u_{i\xi}(v_{i\xi}^*) \ge 0 \end{array} \right\} \tag{6.49}$$

From equation 6.47,

$$\frac{dq_{i\xi}(v_{i\xi}^*)}{dv_{i\xi}} + \mu^* \frac{du_{i\xi}(v_{i\xi}^*)}{dv_{i\xi}} = 0$$

$$(i = 1, 2, \ldots, N, \ \xi = 1, 2, \ldots, n_i) \tag{6.50}$$

The following function called, "efficiency sensitivity function," is defined:

$$r_{i\xi}(v_{i\xi}) = -\frac{dq_{i\xi}(v_{i\xi})}{du_{i\xi}(v_{i\xi})}$$

$$= \frac{\beta_{i\xi}/v_{i\xi}^2 - \left(\dfrac{1}{n_{i\xi}} - 1\right) \gamma_{i\xi} v_{i\xi}^{\frac{1}{n_{i\xi}} - 2} / C_{i\xi}^{\frac{1}{n_{i\xi}}}}{-1/v_{i\xi}^2 + \left(\dfrac{1}{n_{i\xi}} - 1\right) b_{i\xi} v_{i\xi}^{\frac{1}{n_{i\xi}} - 2} / C_{i\xi}^{\frac{1}{n_{i\xi}}}} - \alpha$$

$$(i = 1, 2, \ldots, N, \xi = 1, 2, \ldots, n_i) \qquad (6.51)$$

Since the time function $u_{i\xi}$ and the cost function $q_{i\xi}$ have the minimal points at the maximum-production-rate machining speed $v_{i\xi}^{(t)}$ and the minimum-production-cost machining speed $v_{i\xi}^{(c)}$, respectively, for $v_{i\xi} = v_{i\xi}^{(c)}$ and $v_{i\xi}^{(t)}$

$$r_{i\xi}(v_{i\xi}^{(c)}) = 0$$

and

$$r_{i\xi}(v_{i\xi}^{(t)}) = \infty \qquad (6.52)$$

The derivative of the above function with respect to $v_{i\xi}$ is:

$$\frac{dr_{i\xi}(v_{i\xi})}{dv_{i\xi}} = \frac{1}{n_{i\xi}} \left(\frac{1}{n_{i\xi}} - 1 \right) \left(\frac{\gamma_{i\xi} - b_{i\xi}\beta_{i\xi}}{C_{i\xi}^{\frac{1}{n_{i\xi}}}} \right) v_{i\xi}^{\frac{1}{n_{i\xi}}-5} /$$

$$\left\{ -\frac{1}{v_{i\xi}^2} + \left(\frac{1}{n_{i\xi}} - 1 \right) \frac{b_{i\xi}}{C_{i\xi}^{\frac{1}{n_{i\xi}}}} v_{i\xi}^{\frac{1}{n_{i\xi}}-2} \right\}^2 \qquad (6.53)$$

Generally, in machining of metals, $n_{i\xi}$, parameter of the Taylor tool-life equation, is $0 < n_{i\xi} < 1$, hence, $(1/n_{i\xi}) - 1 > 0$. Since it is assumed previously that the minimum-cost speed $v_{i\xi}^{(c)}$ is less than the minimum-time speed $v_{i\xi}^{(t)}$, from equations 6.28 and 6.32, $\gamma_{i\xi} - b_{i\xi}\beta_{i\xi} > 0$. Therefore, in the speed range $E_{i\xi} = [v_{i\xi}^{(c)}, v_{i\xi}^{(t)}]$, which is called the "high-efficiency range," from equation 6.53,

$$\left. \frac{dr_{i\xi}(v_{i\xi})}{dv_{i\xi}} \right|_{v_{i\xi} \in E_{i\xi}} > 0 \qquad (6.54)$$

It is concluded from the above discussion that the function $r_{i\xi}(v_{i\xi})$ is nonnegative and monotone increasing from 0 to ∞ on $E_{i\xi}$. Consequently, there exists the inverse function of $r_{i\xi}(v_{i\xi})$ for $\mu \geq 0$, which is denoted by $r_{i\xi}^{-1}(\mu) \in E_{i\xi}$.

The above analysis leads to the following proposition.

Proposition 4. For the optimal solution to the nonlinear program expressed in equations 6.44 and 6.45, the following must be satisfied:

1. $\mu^* > 0$ implies $\delta^* = 0$ and $v_{i\xi}^* = r_{i\xi}^{-1}(\mu^*) \in [v_{i\xi}^{(c)}, v_{i\xi}^{(t)}]$.
2. $\mu^* = 0$ implies $\delta^* \geq 0$ and $v_{i\xi}^* = v_{i\xi}^{(c)}$.

6.3.3 *Optimizing Algorithm*

Based on the analytical results mentioned above, the following computational algorithm is proposed for determining the optimal product items and the optimal machining speeds to be set for those items selected.

Step 1. Calculate $v_{i\xi}^{(t)}$ and $p_{i\xi}^{(t)}$ for all i and ξ by equation 6.37, and then Q by equation 6.36. If $Q = d$, go to step 2; if $Q < d$, go to step 3; and if $Q > d$, go to step 4.

Step 2. The optimal solution is:

$$x_{i\xi}^* = 1, \ v_{i\xi}^* = v_{i\xi}^{(t)} \ (i = 1, 2, \ldots, N, \ \xi = 1, 2, \ldots, n_i)$$

$$z^* = z_{\max}$$

Stop.

Step 3. Set an appropriate value $\mu > 0$, and calculate $v_{i\xi}^{(e)} = r_{i\xi}^{-1}(\mu) \in E_{i\xi}$ for all i and ξ, such that $\Sigma_{i=1}^{N}[S_i + \Sigma_{\xi=1}^{n_i}\{s_{i\xi} + l_{i\xi}u_{i\xi}(v_{i\xi}^{(e)})\}] \leq d$, where the inequality sign holds only when $\mu = 0$, in such a case, set $v_{i\xi}^{(e)} = v_{i\xi}^{(c)}$. The optimal solution is:

$$x_{i\xi}^* = 1, \ v_{i\xi}^* = v_{i\xi}^{(e)} \ (i = 1, 2, \ldots, N, \ \xi = 1, 2, \ldots, n_i)$$

$$z^* = z_{\max}$$

The amount of cost reduction is:

$$\Delta y = \sum_{i=1}^{N} \sum_{\xi=1}^{n_i} \{q_{i\xi}(v_{i\xi}^{(t)}) - q_{i\xi}(v_{i\xi}^{(e)})\}$$

Stop.

Step 4. Generate the initial list: $k = 0$, $K = \{k\}$, $R = U$, $S = \phi$, $D = 0$, $\delta = d$, $X_i = 0$ $(i = 1, 2, \ldots, N)$. $\underline{z} = 0$ and $\bar{z} = [\delta/\min_{i\xi \in R}\{(S_i + s_{i\xi})/l_{i\xi} + u_{i\xi}^{(t)}\}]$. Go to step 5.

Step 5. Find $\max_{k \in K} \bar{z}$ and denote such index by $\hat{k}$. For the list $\hat{k}$, if $\underline{z} = \bar{z}$, go to step 10; otherwise, go to step 6.

Step 6. Find $\min_{i\xi \in R}\{S_i(1 - X_i) + s_{i\xi})/l_{i\xi} + u_{i\xi}^{(t)}\}$, and denote such index by $\hat{i}\hat{\xi}$. Calculate $\hat{D} = D + S_i(1 - X_i) + s_{\hat{i}\hat{\xi}} + w_{\hat{i}\hat{\xi}}u_{\hat{i}\hat{\xi}}$, where $1 \leq w_{\hat{i}\hat{\xi}} \leq l_{\hat{i}\hat{\xi}}$. Increase $w_{\hat{i}\hat{\xi}}$ up to $l_{\hat{i}\hat{\xi}}$ as long as $\hat{D} \leq d$; otherwise, replace $l_{\hat{i}\hat{\xi}}$ by $w_{\hat{i}\hat{\xi}}$ which holds the relation: $\hat{D} \leq d \leq \hat{D} + u_{i\xi}^{(t)}$. If $w_{\hat{i}\hat{\xi}} = 0$, go to step 7; if $\hat{D} = d$, go to step 8; and if $D < d$, go to step 9.

Step 7. Set $R = R - \{\hat{i}\hat{\xi}\}$ for the list $\hat{k}$. If $R = \phi$ set $\underline{z} = \bar{z}$. Return to step 5.

Step 8. Generate a new list: $k = k + 1$, $K = K + \{k\} - \{\hat{k}\}$, $S = S + \{\hat{i}\hat{\xi}\}$, $\delta = 0$, $\underline{z} = \underline{z} + w\hat{i}\hat{\xi}$, and $\bar{z} = \underline{z}$. Return to step 5.

Step 9. Branch the list $\hat{k}$ and generate two new lists: $k = k + 1$, $K = K + \{k\} - \{\hat{k}\}$, $R = R - \{\hat{i}\xi\}$, $S = S$, $D = D$, $\delta = \delta$, $\underline{z} = \underline{z}$, and $\bar{z} = \underline{z} + \lceil \delta / \min_{i\xi \in R} [\{S_i(1 - X_i) + s_{i\xi}\}/l_{i\xi} + u_{i\xi}^{(t)}] \rceil$ if $R \neq \phi$, or $\bar{z} = \underline{z}$ if $R = \phi$; and $k = k + 1$, $K = K + \{k\}$, $R = R$, $S = S + \{\hat{i}\xi\}$, $D = \hat{D}$, $\delta = d - D$, $X_i = 1$, $\underline{z} = \underline{z} + w_{i\xi}$ and $\bar{z} = \underline{z} + \lceil \delta / \min_{i\xi \in R} [\{S_i(1 - X_i) + s_{i\xi}\}/l_{i\xi} + u_{i\xi}^{(t)}] \rceil$ if $R \neq \phi$ or $\bar{z} = \underline{z}$ if $R = \phi$. Return to step 5.

Step 10. The optimal solution is obtained in the list $\hat{k}$: By setting $S^* = S$,

$$x_{i\xi}^* = 1, \; v_{i\xi}^* = v_{i\xi}^{(t)} \text{ for all } i\xi \in S^*$$
$$x_{i\xi}^* = 0, \; v_{i\xi}^* = \text{indefinite for all } i\xi \in U - S^*$$
$$z^* = \bar{z}$$

Stop.

Example 6.3. Using the computational algorithm developed in the previous subsection, a numerical example for determining the optimal parts to be made as well as the optimal machining speeds to be utilized for producing the parts are presented. Data for the example are given as shown in table 6.3. The optimal parts to be selected for production in a limited capacity of the machine tool are obtained by the optimizing algorithm, and indicated by "A" in table 6.4. The optimal machining speeds for such selected parts are also presented in table 6.4.

In analyzing the above machine loading problem, the criterion employed was the maximization of the production rate. The problem of the criterion for maximizing the total profit was also analyzed. The optimizing algorithm for determining an optimal product mix and optimal machining speeds was developed based on a similar pattern to the one for maximum production rate.

6.4 Group Machine Loading Model with Variable Processing Times: A Multi-Stage Case

6.4.1 Mathematical Model of Multi-Stage Group Machine Loading Problem

From the standpoint of the group technology concept in the previous section, the machine loading problem of a single-stage production system was analytically treated. In this section, the machine loading problem is extended

Table 6.3. Basic data for the numerical example [5]

			Tool Life Parameters				Time Parameters				Cost Parameters		
Group	Part	Lot Size	Lot Machining Constant	Slope Constant	1-Min Life Machining Speed	Group Setup Time	Lot Setup Time	Preparation Time	Tool Replacement Time	Direct Labor Cost and Overhead	Machining Overhead	Tool Cost
i	j	l_{ij}	λ_{ij}	n_{ij}	C_{ij}	S_{ij}	s_{ij}	a_{ij}	b_{ij}	α	β_{ij}	γ_{ij}
Number	Number	pcs			m/min	min	min/lot	min/pc	min/edge	¢/min	¢/min	¢/edge
1	1	60	707	0.25	350	20.00	19.00	2.50	2.00	15	10	400
	2	50	377	0.25	350		8.00	3.00	3.50	15	25	750
2	1	100	1257	0.33	400	22.00	10.00	3.00	3.00	15	15	600
	2	70	982	0.25	250		9.00	4.00	2.50	15	20	800
	3	40	565	0.20	240		15.00	2.50	2.50	15	15	450
3	1	30	565	0.25	250	15.00	5.00	3.00	3.00	15	30	600
	2	90	626	0.33	300		13.00	5.00	1.50	15	15	500
4	1	40	424	0.20	350	25.00	6.00	4.00	3.50	15	20	450
	2	50	1257	0.25	350		10.00	3.00	4.00	15	20	550
	3	80	524	0.20	200		20.00	2.50	4.50	15	25	600

Note: Allowable time = 50 (hr).

Table 6.4. Optimum solutions for the given numerical example [5]

Group	Number	1			2	3				4	
Part	Number	1	2	1	2	3	1	2	1	2	3
Lot Size	pcs	60	50	100	70	40	30	90	40	50	80
Accept(A) or Reject(R)		A	A	A	R	A	A	R	A	A	A
Optimal Machining Speed	m/min	223	194	220	—	151	144	—	260	188	112
Tool Life	min/edge	6.00	10.50	6.09	—	10.00	9.00	—	14.00	12.00	18.00
Production Amount	pcs	60	50	6	—	40	30	—	60	50	80
Production Time	min/lot	421.86	287.26	79.07	—	311.72	251.71	—	268.71	605.71	686.69
Group Production Time	min	729.12			412.79	266.71				1585.90	
Total Production Amount	pcs	356									

Total production time 2994.52 min

Remaining time 5.48

to the problem of a multi-stage production system [6]. An analysis is made to optimally select parts to be produced and then to determine optimal machining speeds on each of the stages for the parts selected to maximize the production rate.

The product items (jobs) are to be processed on a production system in a flow shop which consists of K stages. The stage index is denoted by $k\,(=1, 2,\ldots,K)$. The time limitation available at stage k (machine M_k) is denoted by $d_k\,(k=1, 2,\ldots,K)$.

The multi-stage group machine loading problem to be solved is to determine the optimal kinds of parts (or jobs) to be produced within limited times available to multi-stages as well as to decide the optimal machining speeds on each stage for the parts selected. Two kinds of criteria are employed for the problem defined. The primary criterion is the maximization of the production rate and the secondary one is the minimization of the production cost.

The primary objective function is to:
Maximize

$$z = \sum_{i=1}^{N} \sum_{\xi=1}^{n_i} w_{i\xi} x_{i\xi} \qquad (6.55)$$

where $w_{i\xi}$ is the accepted amount of $J_{i\xi}$ (the ξth job in group $i(G_i)$) and is given by $0 \le w_{i\xi} \le l_{i\xi}(l_{i\xi}$: lot size of $J_{i\xi})$.

The secondary one is to minimize

$$C = \sum_{i=1}^{N} \sum_{\xi=1}^{n_i} \sum_{k=1}^{K} w_{i\xi} q_{i\xi}^{k} x_{i\xi} \qquad (6.56)$$

where $q_{i\xi}^{k}$ is the unit production cost for $J_{i\xi}$ on stage $k(M_k)$.

The following constraints must be satisfied when solving the multi-stage group machine loading problem defined, because the available time of each stage is limited as $d_k(k=1, 2,\ldots,K)$.

$$\sum_{i=1}^{N} \left(S_i^k X_i + \sum_{\xi=1}^{n_i} p_{i\xi}^{k} x_{i\xi} \right) \le d_k \qquad (6.57)$$

where S_i^k is the group setup time for G_i on M_k and $p_{i\xi}^{k}$ is the job processing time for $J_{i\xi}$ on M_k.

The multi-stage group machine loading problem is now formulated to first maximize equation 6.55 and then to minimize equation 6.56 subject to equation 6.57.

6.4.2 Analysis of Multi-Stage Group Machine Loading Model

The time needed to produce all the parts at the minimum-time machining speed for each stage is given by:

$$Q^k = \sum_{i=1}^{N} \left\{ S_i^k + \sum_{\xi=1}^{n_i} \left(s_{i\xi}^k + l_{i\xi} u_{i\xi}^{k(t)} \right) \right\} \qquad (6.58)$$

where $s_{i\xi}^k$ is job setup time for $J_{i\xi}$ on M_k and $u_{i\xi}^{k(t)}$ is the minimum time for $J_{i\xi}$ on M_k; that is, the production time at the minimum-time machining speed, $v_{i\xi}^{k(t)}$ for $J_{i\xi}$ on M_k.

Then the following three cases are considered:

1. Case 1: $Q^k = d_k \ (\forall k)$
2. Case 2: $Q^k \leq d_k \ (\forall k)$
3. Case 3: $Q^k > d_k \ (\exists k)$

Let us consider each of three cases.

Case 1: In this case, it is evident that the optimal solution is given by:

$$\left. \begin{aligned} & x_{i\xi}^* = 1 \ (i = 1, 2, \ldots, N, \xi = 1, 2, \ldots, n_i) \\ & v_{i\xi}^{k*} = v_{i\xi}^{k(t)} \ \begin{pmatrix} i = 1, 2, \ldots, N, \xi = 1, 2, \ldots, n_i \\ k = 1, 2, \ldots, K \end{pmatrix} \\ & z^* = \sum_{i=1}^{N} \sum_{\xi=1}^{n_i} l_{i\xi} \ (\equiv z_{\max}) \end{aligned} \right\} \qquad (6.59)$$

Case 2: In this case, all the parts under consideration can be accepted, that is:

$$\left. \begin{aligned} & x_{i\xi}^* = 1 \ (i = 1, 2, \ldots, N, \xi = 1, 2, \ldots, n_i) \\ & z^* = z_{\max} \end{aligned} \right\} \qquad (6.60)$$

The optimal machining speeds are determined as follows: Let K' and K'' denote the set of k such that $Q^k = d_k$ and the set of k such that $Q^k < d_k$ respectively. For stage k $(k \in K')$, the optimal machining speeds are given by:

$$v_{i\xi}^{k*} = v_{i\xi}^{k(t)}$$

$$(i = 1, 2, \ldots, N, \xi = 1, 2, \ldots, n_i, k \in K') \qquad (6.61)$$

With the use of slack time $(d_k - Q^k)$ on stage k ($k \in K''$), the production cost, which is a secondary objective function to be minimized, can be reduced by decreasing the machining speed on that stage from the minimum-production-time machining speed.

The problem is to minimize

$$C = \sum_{i=1}^{N} \sum_{\xi=1}^{n_i} l_{i\xi} q_{i\xi}^k(v_{i\xi}^k) \tag{6.62}$$

subject to

$$\sum_{i=1}^{N} \left[S_i^k + \sum_{\xi=1}^{n_i} p_{i\xi}^k (v_{i\xi}^k) \right] \leq d_k, \, k \in K'' \tag{6.63}$$

Applying the Kuhn-Tucker's theorem to this problem, nonnegative constants μ_k^*, which satisfy the following conditions, exist for the optimal machining speeds $v_{i\xi}^k$

$$\sum \sum l_{i\xi} \frac{dq_{i\xi}^k(v_{i\xi}^{k*})}{dv_{i\xi}^k} + \mu_k^* \sum_{i=1}^{N} \sum_{\xi=1}^{n_i} l_{i\xi} \frac{dp_{i\xi}^k(v_{i\xi}^{k*})}{dv_{i\xi}^k} = 0, \, k \in K'' \tag{6.64}$$

$$\mu_k^* \left[d_k - \sum_{i=1}^{N} \left\{ S_i^k + \sum_{\xi=1}^{n_i} (s_{i\xi}^k + l_{i\xi} u_{i\xi}^k(v_{i\xi}^{k*})) \right\} \right] = \mu_k^* \delta_k^* = 0, \, k \in K'' \tag{6.65}$$

$$\delta_k^* = d_k - \sum_{i=1}^{N} \left\{ S_i^k + \sum_{\xi=1}^{n_i} (s_{i\xi}^k + l_{i\xi} u_{i\xi}^k(v_{i\xi}^{k*})) \right\} \geq 0, \, k \in K'' \tag{6.66}$$

Then the following function which was defined by equation 6.51 in the previous section is introduced.

$$r_{i\xi}^k(v_{i\xi}^k) = -\frac{dq_{i\xi}^k(v_{i\xi}^k)}{du_{i\xi}^k(v_{i\xi}^k)} \tag{6.67}$$

By utilizing the fact that there exists a unique inverse function of $r_{i\xi}(v_{i\xi}^k)$ for $\mu_k > 0$, the following conclusions are reached.

1. In the cases that $\delta_k^* > 0$ (which implies $\mu_k^* = 0$) and that $\delta_k^* \mu_k^* = 0$ Denoting by K_1'', the set of k in these cases, then

$$v_{i\xi}^{k*} = r_{i\xi}^k(0)^{-1} = v_{i\xi}^{k(c)}, \ k \in K''_1 \qquad (6.68)$$

2. In the case that $\delta_k^* = 0$ and $\mu_k^* > 0$. Denoting by K''_2 the set of k in this case, then

$$v_{i\xi}^{k*} = r_{i\xi}^k(\mu_k^*)^{-1} = v_{i\xi}^{k(e)}, \ k \in K''_2 \qquad (6.69)$$

where $v_{i\xi}^{k(e)}$ is a high-efficiency machining speed which lies in the range $E_{i\xi}^k = [v_{i\xi}^{k(c)}, v_{i\xi}^{k(t)}]$.

Case 3: Let K''' denote the set of k such that $Q^k > d_k$. In this case, some parts cannot be accepted, hence $z^* < z_{\max}$. The problem of determining the parts to be selected is replaced by the following 0-1 type linear program.
Maximize equation 6.55 subject to

$$\sum_{i=1}^{N} \left[S_i^k X_i + \sum_{\xi=1}^{n_i} (s_{i\xi}^k + w_{i\xi} u_{i\xi}^{k(t)}) x_{i\xi} \right] \leq d_k, \ k \in K''' \qquad (6.70)$$

In this problem, the machining speeds, $v_{i\xi}^k$ are no longer decision variables since they are set at the minimum-production-time speeds and are constants. In order to determine the optimal solution for this problem, the branch-and-bound method is employed. This method consists of two fundamental procedures: branching and bounding procedures.

The branching procedure to partition a solution set into several subsets is as follows:

Among the nodes (of level r and s) at which the accept-reject decisions are made as to r groups of N, the node with the maximum upper bound $\bar{z}$ (which is calculated in the bounding procedure) (in the case of a tie, select the node with the largest value of first r and then s.) is partitioned such that a new part is accepted as a candidate or rejected.

The bounding procedure calculates the lower and upper bounds on the number of parts to be accepted at each node. The upper and lower bounds are estimated as follows:

$$\bar{z} = \sum_{i\xi \in S} l_{i\xi} x_{i\xi} + \min_{k \in K''} \left[\delta_k / \min_{i\xi \in R} \left\{ \frac{S_i^k(1 - X_i) + s_{i\xi}^k}{l_{i\xi}} + u_{i\xi}^{k(t)} \right\} \right] \qquad (6.71)$$

$$\underline{z} = \sum_{i\xi \in S} l_{i\xi} x_{i\xi} + \min_{k \in K''} \left[\delta_k / \max_{i\xi \in R} \left\{ \frac{S_i^k(1 - X_i) + s_{i\xi}^k}{l_{i\xi}} + u_{i\xi}^{k(t)} \right\} \right] \qquad (6.72)$$

where S and R are the sets of subscripts of parts that will be accepted or not, respectively. $\lceil\ \rceil$ stands for a Gaussian notation, and

$$\delta_k = d_k - \sum_{i \in S} S_i^k - \sum_{i\xi \in S} (s_{i\xi}^k + l_{i\xi} u_{i\xi}^{k(t)}) \qquad (6.73)$$

The termination rule for this procedure is that at a selected node there exists a stage index $k \in K''$ such that $\delta_k \leq 0$. At that node, set $\underline{z} = \bar{z}$ and the remaining parts are not accepted.

At the node with max $\bar{z}$ and with $\bar{z} = \underline{z}$, the optimal solution is obtained. Denoting S^* the set of parts accepted at that node, then

$$x_{i\xi}^* = \begin{cases} 1 \text{ if } i\xi \in S^* \\ 0 \text{ if } i\xi \notin S^* \end{cases} \qquad (6.74)$$

Thus the value of the primal objective function is:

$$z^* = \bar{z} \qquad (6.75)$$

The optimal machining speeds for the parts selected are determined by solving the following subproblem:

Maximize

$$z_k = \sum_{i\xi \in S^*} w_{i\xi} q_{i\xi}^k(v_{i\xi}^k)$$

subject to

$$\left. \begin{array}{l} \\ \sum_{i\xi \in S^*} w_{i\xi} p_{i\xi}^k(v_{i\xi}^k) \leq d_k' \\ \\ d_k' = d_k - \sum_{i\xi \in S^*} (S_i^k + s_{i\xi}^k)\ (k = 1, 2, \ldots, K) \end{array} \right\} \qquad (6.76)$$

This problem is just the same type as one for case 2. Therefore, the optimal machining speeds can be determined in the same way.

Example 6.4. In an attempt to clarify the multistage machine-loading problem, a numerical example is presented. Production data for the example are given in table 6.5. With the use of a solution procedure developed above, the optimal parts to be selected for production data are given in table 6.6. The branching tree for determining this solution is given in figure 6.1. The figures just below the nodes indicate the upper bounds pertaining to the number of parts to be selected. For example, the upper bound at job node J_{43} is calculated through table 6.7 and figure 6.2.

At the branching from job node J_{11} having the upper bound of 333, there occurs a stage index $k \in K''$ such that $\delta_k < 0$; hence the entire lot of any other

Table 6.5. Production data for multi-stage group machine loading [7]

(a)

Group G_i	Job J_{ij}	Lot w_{ij}	Processing Parameter — Cutting Parameter λ_{ij}^k	Tool Parameter — 1-Min Tool Life Speed C_{ij}^k (m/min)	Tool Parameter — Slope Constant $n_{i\xi}^k$	Time Parameter — Job Setup Time $s_{i\xi}^k$ (min)	Time Parameter — Preparation Time $a_{i\xi}^k$ (min/pc)	Time Parameter — Tool Exchange Time $b_{i\xi}^k$ (min/edge)	Cost Parameter — Direct Labor Cost and Overhead $\alpha_{i\xi}^k$ ($/min)	Cost Parameter — Machining Overhead Cost $\beta_{i\xi}^k$ ($/min)	Cost Parameter — Tool Cost $\gamma_{i\xi}^k$ ($/edge)
G_1	J_{11}	50	707	350	0.25	8	2.5	2.0	0.15	0.10	8
			471	200	0.20	10	3.0	3.5	0.20	0.25	15
			1257	400	0.33	15	3.0	3.0	0.17	0.15	12
			660	250	0.25	13	4.0	2.5	0.22	0.20	16
	J_{12}	40	293	340	0.20	7	2.5	2.5	0.15	0.15	9
			550	250	0.25	15	3.0	3.0	0.20	0.30	12
			589	300	0.33	12	5.0	1.5	0.17	0.15	10
			424	350	0.20	7	4.0	3.5	0.22	0.20	9.5
G_2	J_{21}	80	1257	350	0.25	12	3.0	4.0	0.15	0.20	9.5
			524	200	0.20	7	2.5	4.5	0.20	0.10	12
			943	320	0.33	7	3.5	3.5	0.17	0.10	13
			365	250	0.22	6	4.0	2.0	0.22	0.15	11.5
	J_{22}	50	1932	400	0.20	10	3.0	5.0	0.15	0.40	11.5
			1178	300	0.25	9	3.5	3.5	0.20	0.35	12.5
			330	250	0.33	9	4.0	2.0	0.17	0.30	9
			905	350	0.20	15	5.0	4.0	0.22	0.25	14

	J_{23}	30	1491	400	0.20	7	4.0	4.0	0.15	0.25	9
			884	380	0.33	6	3.0	4.5	0.20	0.30	12.5
			1571	330	0.25	8	3.5	3.0	0.17	0.20	14
			777	280	0.23	10	4.5	3.5	0.22	0.35	11.5
G_3	J_{31}	60	550	300	0.20	9	4.0	5.0	0.15	0.15	9
			1060	250	0.33	11	3.5	2.0	0.20	0.10	14
			707	340	0.25	6	2.5	5.5	0.17	0.10	13.5
			1089	270	0.23	10	2.0	3.0	0.22	0.25	15
	J_{41}	70	707	350	0.20	14	3.5	5.0	0.15	0.20	12
			648	200	0.25	9	4.0	3.0	0.20	0.25	13.5
			354	200	0.20	7	2.0	3.0	0.17	0.25	14.5
			471	250	0.22	9	3.0	4.0	0.22	0.10	9
	J_{42}	40	715	400	0.25	8	4.0	3.5	0.15	0.20	6.5
			335	250	0.20	7	3.0	4.0	0.20	0.30	13.5
			534	500	0.33	15	3.5	2.0	0.17	0.20	12.5
			312	320	0.20	12	2.5	3.0	0.22	0.25	14
G_4	J_{43}	50	792	500	0.25	9	5.0	2.5	0.15	0.15	7.5
			660	400	0.20	13	4.5	4.0	0.20	0.25	12.5
			469	350	0.25	12	3.0	3.0	0.17	0.30	10.5
			354	280	0.33	7	5.0	2.0	0.22	0.40	13
	J_{44}	70	1045	300	0.20	13	5.0	2.5	0.15	0.15	7.5
			1021	340	0.25	9	3.5	3.0	0.20	0.32	9.5
			1485	250	0.33	10	4.5	4.0	0.17	0.20	12
			563	400	0.20	9	3.0	3.5	0.22	0.35	10

(continued on next page)

Table 6.5 (*continued*)

		(b)
Group	*Stage*	*Group Setup Time*
G_i	M_k	S_i^k (min)
G_1	M_1	26.0
	M_2	20.0
	M_3	24.0
	M_4	21.0
G_2	M_1	28.0
	M_2	19.0
	M_3	23.0
	M_4	22.0
G_3	M_1	20.0
	M_2	18.0
	M_3	19.0
	M_4	25.0
G_4	M_1	18.0
	M_2	25.0
	M_3	21.0
	M_4	24.0

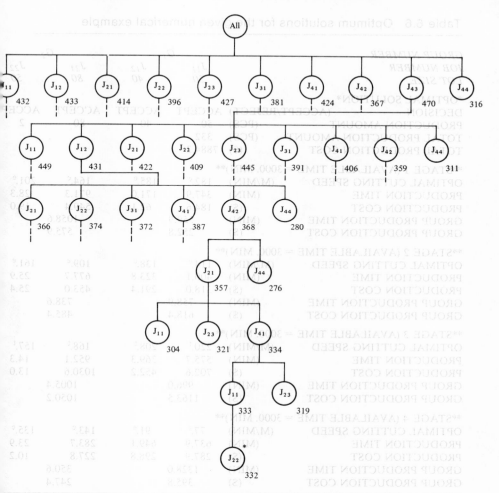

Figure 6.1. The branching tree for the multi-stage group machine loading problem

Table 6.6   Optimum solutions for the given numerical example

GROUP NUMBER		G_1		G_2	
JOB NUMBER		J_{11}	J_{12}	J_{21}	J_{22}
LOT SIZE		50	40	80	50
OPTIMAL SOLUTION					
DECISION (ACCEPT/REJECT)		ACCEPT	ACCEPT	ACCEPT	ACCEP
PRODUCTION AMOUNT	(PCS)	50	40	80	2
TOTAL PRODUCTION AMOUNT	(PCS)	332			
TOTAL PRODUCTION COST	($)	7884.2			
STAGE 1 (AVAILABLE TIME = 3000. MIN)					
OPTIMAL CUTTING SPEED	(M/MIN)	182.[e]	185.[e]	164.[e]	201.[e]
PRODUCTION TIME	(MIN)	347.9	171.0	971.3	28.3
PRODUCTION COST	($)	184.6	62.1	549.4	19.0
GROUP PRODUCTION TIME	(MIN)	559.9		1058.6	
GROUP PRODUCTION COST	($)	252.8		575.9	
STAGE 2 (AVAILABLE TIME = 3000. MIN)					
OPTIMAL CUTTING SPEED	(M/MIN)	114.[e]	138.[e]	109.[e]	161.[e]
PRODUCTION TIME	(MIN)	400.1	323.8	677.7	25.9
PRODUCTION COST	($)	318.0	291.4	453.0	25.4
GROUP PRODUCTION TIME	(MIN)	758.9		738.6	
GROUP PRODUCTION COST	($)	618.4		485.4	
STAGE 3 (AVAILABLE TIME = 3000. MIN)					
OPTIMAL CUTTING SPEED	(M/MIN)	220.[t]	208.[t]	168.[t]	157.[t]
PRODUCTION TIME	(MIN)	575.7	369.3	952.1	14.3
PRODUCTION COST	($)	702.6	452.2	1030.6	13.0
GROUP PRODUCTION TIME	(MIN)	996.0		1005.4	
GROUP PRODUCTION COST	($)	1163.5		1050.2	
STAGE 4 (AVAILABLE TIME = 3000. MIN)					
OPTIMAL CUTTING SPEED	(M/MIN)	77.[e]	91.[e]	143.[e]	135.[e]
PRODUCTION TIME	(MIN)	637.9	649.1	283.7	23.9
PRODUCTION COST	($)	287.9	298.8	227.8	10.2
GROUP PRODUCTION TIME	(MIN)	1328.0		350.6	
GROUP PRODUCTION COST	($)	395.8		247.4	

Note: The symbols [t], [c], and [e] above the machining speeds indicate the maximum-production-machining speeds, the minimum-cost machining speeds, and the machining speeds in the high-efficie speed range, respectively. [7]

J_{23} 30	G_3 J_{31} 60	J_{41} 70	G_4 J_{42} 40	J_{43} 50	J_{44} 70
REJECT	REJECT	ACCEPT	ACCEPT	ACCEPT	REJECT
—	—	70	40	50	—
—	—	172.[e]	198.[e]	256.[e]	—
—	—	573.8	334.7	431.2	—
—	—	243.0	124.1	167.8	—
	—		1388.7		
	—		542.2		
—	—	110.[e]	140.[e]	224.[e]	—
—	—	805.9	236.8	404.8	—
—	—	766.9	146.5	218.8	—
	—		1501.5		
	—		1142.9		
—	—	122.[t]	315.[t]	202.[t]	—
—	—	394.6	241.3	304.7	—
—	—	364.1	263.4	222.0	—
	—		995.6		
	—		858.8		
—	—	91.[e]	124.[e]	81.[c]	—
—	—	587.0	203.5	477.9	—
—	—	198.3	82.2	259.0	—
	—		1320.4		
	—		550.9		

Table 6.7(a). Calculate upper bound at job node J_{43} [7]

	Job	J_{11}	J_{12}	J_{21}	J_{22}	J_{23}	J_{31}	J_{41}	J_{42}	J_{44}
STAGE 1	$S_i^k(1-X_i)+s_{i\xi}^k$	0.680	0.825	0.500	0.760	1.167	1.450	0.200	0.200	0.186
	$l_{i\xi}$ $u_{i\xi}^k$	6.7	4.2	11.9	14.0	12.1	8.2	8.1	8.3	11.9
	Total	7.380	5.025 *	12.400	14.760	13.267	9.65	8.300	8.500	12.086
STAGE 2	$S_i^k(1-X_i)+s_{i\xi}^k$	0.600	0.875	0.325	0.560	0.833	1.450	0.129	0.175	0.129
	$l_{i\xi}$ $u_{i\xi}^k$	8.0	8.1	8.3	12.9	10.2	13.6	11.5	5.9	10.4
	Total	8.600	8.975	8.625	13.460	11.033	15.05	11.629	6.075 *	10.529
STAGE 3	$S_i^k(1-X_i)+s_{i\xi}^k$	0.784	0.900	0.375	0.640	1.033	1.250	0.100	0.375	0.143
	$l_{i\xi}$ $u_{i\xi}^k$	11.5	9.2	11.9	7.1	14.5	8.1	5.7	6.0	22.2
	Total	12.284	10.100	12.275	7.740	15.533	9.350	5.800 *	6.375	22.343
STAGE 4	$S_i^k(1-X_i)+s_{i\xi}^k$	0.680	0.700	0.350	0.740	1.067	1.750	0.129	0.300	0.129
	$l_{i\xi}$ $u_{i\xi}^k$	9.8	14.6	6.9	10.6	10.9	10.9	7.3	4.5	6.0
	Total	10.480	15.300	7.250	11.340	11.967	12.650	7.429	4.800 *	6.129

Table 6.7(b).   Calculate upper bound at job node J_{43} [7]

Stage K (1)	$\sum_{i\xi\in S} l_{i\xi}x_{i\xi}$ (2) (pcs)	Available Time (3) (min)	δ_k (4) (min)	$\min_{i\xi\in R}\left\{\dfrac{S_i^k(1-X_i)+s_{i\xi}^k}{l_{i\xi}}+u_{i\xi}^k\right\}$ (5) (min)	$\left\lceil \dfrac{(4)}{(5)} \right\rceil$ (6) (pcs)
1	50 (lot size of J_{43})	3000	2548	5.025	507
2	50	3000	2557	6.075	420 (minimum)
3	50	3000	2662	5.800	458
4	50	3000	2569	4.800	535

Note: Upper bound = 50 + 420 = 470.

Figure 6.2.   Calculating upper bound at job node J_4 [7]

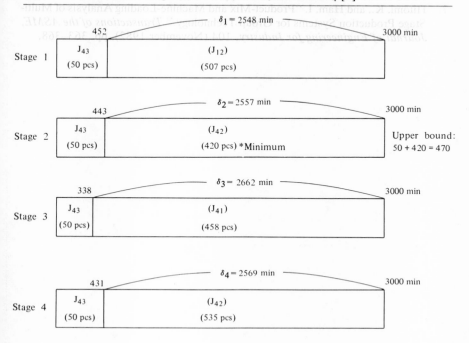

job can be accepted no longer. Then job J_{22} having the largest efficiency sensitivity function is selected and two parts of the job are accepted, considering the slack time of each stage.

REFERENCES

1. Hitomi, K. *Manufacturing Systems Engineering*. London: Taylor & Francis Ltd., pp. 167–173, 1978.
2. Hitomi, K. "Analysis of Production Model: Part 1: The Optimal Decision of Production Speed." *AIIE Transactions*, 8(1), pp. 96–105, 1976.
3. Hitomi, K. "Analysis of Production Model: Part 2: Optimization of a Multistage Production System." *AIIE Transactions*, 8(1), pp. 106–112, 1976.
4. Kuhn, H. W., and Tucher, A. W. "Nonlinear Programming." *Proceedings of the Second Berkeley Symposium on Mathematical Statistics and Probability*, edited by J. Neyman, Berkeley: University of California Press, pp. 481–492, 1950.
5. Hitomi, K., and Ham, I. "Machine Loading and Product-Mix Analysis for Group Technology." *Transactions of the ASME, Journal of Engineering for Industry*, 100 (August 1978), pp. 370–374.
6. Ham, I., and Hitomi, K. "Group Technology Applications for Machine Loading Under Multi-Resource Constraints." pp. 515–518, *9th NAMRC* 1981.
7. Hitomi, K., and Ham, I. "Product-Mix and Machine-Loading Analysis of Multi-Stage Production Systems for Group Technology." *Transactions of the ASME, Journal of Engineering for Industry*, 104 (November 1982), pp. 363–368.

7 PRODUCTION SCHEDULING FOR GROUP TECHNOLOGY

7.1 Essentials of Production Scheduling

Product items and their quantities to be produced in the specified periods are determined through production planning. Then an actual implementation plan as to the time schedule for performing required jobs must be established; that is, when, on which machine or work center, and who does what operation. Whether the production activities in a work shop—such as part supply, machining, inspection, and so forth—are performed smoothly or not depends on the time schedule established. When this time schedule is well established, production activities are done smoothly, throughput times of jobs become short, and all the jobs meet their due dates. On the contrary, when badly established, the operations of the jobs may not be performed on the time schedule.

Production scheduling is a function of determining an optimal or near-optimal implementation time schedule for performing necessary jobs. Except for rare cases, it is difficult to determine an optimal schedule in a real situation in a short period of time. The reason lies in the difficulty of acquiring accurate information concerning jobs to be processed and concerns production capacities such as production facilities, manpower, and so forth. Even if the up-to-date and accurate information is completely available,

93

determining an optimal schedule in a short time is not easy because in actual cases the number of schedules to be considered is not small.

The task of establishing the time schedule for jobs is basically that of determining the sequence of processing jobs on each machine. Assuming that n jobs are processed on a single machine, there exist $n!$ alternatives. Moreover, in the case of processing n jobs on m machines, it may be possible that there are $(n!)^m$ alternatives. Among them, an optimal sequence according to a certain measure of performance definitely exists and can be theoretically found in a finite number of computational iterations. However, it requires a lot of computational efforts, particularly as the number of jobs and machines become large. For example, there are $(8!)^3 \doteq 6.6 \times 10^{13}$ alternatives for even a relatively small problem such as eight jobs on three machines. Hence, it is not practical to evaluate all the alternatives according to a certain measure of performance and then find an optimal one even when using a high-speed computer. Thus we need a good method or algorithm for finding an optimal schedule without enumerating all possible alternatives.

In general, a job consists of a given sequence of operations predecided by the production's technological order. The processing of an operation requires the use of a particular machine for a given duration—processing time of the operation. When the sequence of machines on which operations of each job are performed is completely identical for all jobs, this shop is called a "flow shop," and production scheduling for this shop is called "flow-shop scheduling." This type of flow pattern is typical for mass production. In case of jobbing production or small- and medium-sized lot production, the technological sequence of machines for each job is mostly different depending on types of jobs. This type of shop is called a "job shop" and production scheduling for such a job shop is called "job-shop scheduling."

7.2 Basic Models of Production Scheduling

7.2.1 Production Scheduling Models

The purpose of production scheduling is to determine an optimal schedule or near-optimal schedule in small computation efforts. To achieve this purpose, many production scheduling models have been hitherto constructed. Through theoretical analyses based on these models, effective theorems, rules, and algorithms for determining optimal or near optimal schedules have been developed.

Basic production scheduling models are characterized by the following conditions [1,2]:

1. Jobs to be produced are available simultaneously for processing at time zero (a static case).
2. Each machine is continuously available for processing jobs at any time.
3. Jobs consist of a strictly ordered sequence of operations (production-technological order).
4. The time required to complete a job consists of setup time and processing time. It is deterministic and is known in advance based on production technology.
5. Each operation can be performed by only one machine.
6. There is only one machine of each type in the workshop.
7. Preemption is not allowed; that is, once processing begins on a job, it is processed to completion without interruption.
8. The processing times of successive operations of a particular job may not be overlapped.
9. Each machine can handle at most one operation at a time.
10. Intermediate transportation times are ignored or included in processing times.

Several of these assumptions, of course, have frequently been relaxed and other assumptions can be added to these, which results in a different scheduling model.

In general, there may be a number of schedules (sequences) in scheduling a given set of jobs on machines. Therefore, it is necessary to select one or several schedules among them, according to a certain measure of performance. This measure of performance is usually called "scheduling criterion" or simply "criterion." Many kinds of scheduling criteria are employed in production scheduling. The most representative ones include: makespan (total elapsed time), mean flow time, total tardiness, facility utilization in the workshop, et cetera. In some cases, scheduling problems are solved to meet two performance measures; one is a primary criterion, and the other is a secondary one.

In production scheduling problems, there are relatively easy ways to find an optimal solution, while there are also quite hard ones. The most important thing for solving scheduling problems is the efficiency of a solution algorithm, a procedure for obtaining an optimal solution. Recently, scheduling problems have been analyzed and classified from the viewpoint of the problem complexity [3]. In general, the complexity of an algorithm refers to its execution time for finding a solution, which is usually expressed as a function of the number of jobs, n. For our purpose, we need only to concentrate on the terms of a function that dominate the behavior of the execution time, which is called the "order-of-magnitude notation $0(.)$." An algorithm is said to have complexity $0(n^3)$ when there exists a constant c such that the function cn^3 bounds the execution time as a function of n. A solution algorithm whose complexity is bounded by a polynomial in n is a polynomial-time algorithm. The corresponding scheduling problem is said to have a polynomial-time solution (algorithm). A polynomial-time algorithm is considered to be efficient and problems having such an algorithm are easy to solve. However, in the field of production scheduling, there are relatively few problems that have been shown to have polynomial-time algorithms. On the other hand, there is a huge class of problems for which no polynomial-time algorithm has been known. Such problems are called "NP (Non-Polynomial) complete." In addition to production scheduling, well-known problems such as the traveling salesman problem, knapsack problem, and so forth are NP complete [3]. It is said that when one of the NP complete problems is solved, we can find a polynomial-time algorithm for every NP complete problem.

Generally speaking, single-machine scheduling problems seem easy to solve. Certainly many of them are tractable and have polynomial-time algorithms. However, it is also true that some of them are known as NP complete. The flow-shop scheduling problems are relatively tractable because of the simplicity of their job flow patterns. On the other hand, it is quite difficult to determine an optimal schedule for the job-shop scheduling problems where job flow patterns are not identical. Of course, there are a few problems of special structure, such as two-machine flow-shop scheduling and two-job job-shop scheduling, which have polynomial-time algorithms. However, judging from the problem complexity, general flow-shop and job-shop scheduling problems are mostly included in NP complete problems.

7.2.2 Scheduling Criteria

Basic information for production scheduling problems of scheduling n jobs to be processed on m machines is: processing time p_{ij}, required for jth operation of job $i(J_i)$ $(i = 1, 2, \ldots, n, j = 1, 2, \ldots, m_i)$, ready time r_i, the time at which J_i is available, due date d_i, the time at which J_i is due to be completed, where m_i is the number of stages to complete J_i.

The completion time of J_i, the time at which the processing of the last operation of the job is completed is:

$$C_i = r_i + (w_{i1} + p_{i1}) + (w_{i2} + p_{i2}) + \ldots + (w_{im_i} + p_{im_i})$$
$$= r_i + W_i + p_i \tag{7.1}$$

where w_{ij} is the waiting time preceding the jth operation of J_i, W_i is the total waiting time for J_i and is expressed as $\sum_{j=1}^{m_i} w_{ij}$, and p_i is the total processing time of J_i ($\sum_{j=1}^{m_i} p_{ij}$).

The completion time of J_i, that is, the total time length that the job spends in the shop is:

$$F_i = C_i - r_i \qquad (7.2)$$

In this chapter, for simplicity of analysis, the ready times of all jobs are assumed to be zero (static case). Hence, $F_i = C_i$ ($i = 1, 2, \ldots, n$).

In some cases, jobs do not have equal importance. A value or weighting factor, w_i ($i = 1, 2, \ldots, n$) is given for each job to describe its relative importance. The weighted flow time of J_i is:

$$F_{wi} = w_i F_i \qquad (7.3)$$

The weighted mean flow time is:

$$\overline{F}_w = \frac{1}{n} \sum_{i=1}^{n} w_i F_i \qquad (7.4)$$

The makespan (total elapsed time or maximum flow time)—that is, the time length from the beginning of the first operation of the first job to the ending of the last operation of the last job—is:

$$F_{max} = \max_{1 \le i \le n} F_i \qquad (7.5)$$

This is a most important criterion employed in production scheduling.

The mean flow time—that is, the mean time length during which all jobs remain in the shop—is given by:

$$\overline{F} = \frac{1}{n} \sum_{i=1}^{n} F_i \qquad (7.6)$$

The lateness of J_i—that is, the difference of the completion time and the due date—is expressed as:

$$L_i = C_i - d_i \qquad (7.7)$$

Then the tardiness of J_i, a positive amount of lateness, is expressed as:

$$T_i = \max(0, L_i) \qquad (7.8)$$

The maximum lateness and tardiness are, respectively given by:

$$L_{max} = \max_{1 \le i \le n} L_i \qquad (7.9)$$

$$T_{max} = \max_{1 \le i \le n} T_i \qquad (7.10)$$

The total tardiness is expressed as

$$T = \sum_{i=1}^{n} T_i \qquad (7.11)$$

Each of these functions is a function of the completion times of jobs. If the general form expressed as

$$z = f(C_1, C_2, \ldots, C_n) \qquad (7.12)$$

is a function that increases only if at least one of the completion times increases, it is called a "regular measure of performance." The makespan, the mean flow time, the maximum lateness, the maximum tardiness, and the total tardiness are included in this class.

7.2.3 A Single-Machine Scheduling: Job Sequencing

A most basic production scheduling problem is a single-machine (or single-stage) scheduling one in which jobs, each of which consists of a single operation, are processed on a single machine. This situation occurs when many jobs are waiting for processing prior to a machine tool, when many programs are waiting for processing in front of a computer, when an entire plant can be regarded as a single machine, et cetera. In the case of processing n jobs on a single-machine, the total number of distinct schedules (sequences) to be evaluated is $n!$, which is the number of different permutations of n elements. Since a schedule is completely specified by giving the order in which n jobs will be processed, this problem is often called "job sequencing".

In job sequencing, the makespan F_{max} is no longer a suitable scheduling criterion since it is simply the sum of the processing times of jobs:

$$F_{max} = \sum_{i=1}^{n} p_i \qquad (7.13)$$

This value is not dependent on the order of jobs, if all processing times are constant. In the case of sequence-dependent processing time, however, the makespan is dependent on the order of jobs. This problem is similar to a traveling salesman problem for which a useful solution algorithm has been developed by Little et al. [4].

With respect to other scheduling criteria, the following theorems hold.

Theorem 7.1. In the single-machine scheduling problem, the mean flow time is minimized by sequencing the jobs in order of nondecreasing processing times.

Sequencing the jobs in nondecreasing order of processing time is called "shortest-processing-time (SPT)" sequencing. This plays a critical role in production scheduling—even in dynamic production scheduling problems where jobs arrive at shop at random times.

Theorem 7.2 In the single-machine scheduling problem, the maximum lateness and maximum tardiness are minimized by sequencing the jobs in order of nondecreasing due dates.

Sequencing the jobs in nondecreasing order of due date is called "earliest-due-date (EDD)" sequencing.

Theorem 7.3 In the single-machine scheduling problem, if there exists a sequence such that the maximum tardiness is zero, then an optimal sequence minimizing the mean flow time (under the condition that the maximum tardiness remains zero) is obtained by iteratively assigning job J at the last position in the optimal sequence only if

$$\left.\begin{array}{c} (1) \ d_J \geq \displaystyle\sum_{i=1}^{n'} p_i \\[2em] (2) \ p_J \geq p_j \text{ for all jobs with } d_j \geq \displaystyle\sum_{i=1}^{n'} p_i \end{array}\right\} \quad (7.14)$$

where n' is the number of jobs not yet assigned.

Example 7.1 Consider a five-job, single-machine scheduling problem as shown in table 7.1.

In this case, the makespan is invariable ($=16$ days), irrespective of the order of the five jobs.

According to theorem 7.1, the optimal job sequence minimizing the mean flow time is decided as $J_3 - J_1 - J_4 - J_2 - J_5$, which is the SPT schedule. The mean flow time of this sequence is computed as:

$$\bar{F} = [1 + (1 + 2) + (1 + 2 + 3) + (1 + 2 + 3 + 4)$$
$$+ (1 + 2 + 3 + 4 + 6)]/5 = 7.2$$

According to theorem 7.2, the sequence minimizing the maximum

Table 7.1. Basic Data for a Single-Machine Scheduling Problem

Job	J_i	J_1	J_2	J_3	J_4	J_5
Processing time	p_i	2	4	1	3	6
Due date	d_i	18	17	5	7	12

tardiness is the EDD schedule; that is, $J_3 - J_4 - J_5 - J_2 - J_1$, which has the maximum tardiness of zero. Hence, theorem 7.3 can be applied to the problem to obtain a better sequence minimizing the mean flow time under the condition that $T_{max} = 0$. The sequence is obtained as follows: the sum of the processing times is 16. Only jobs J_1 and J_2 have due dates not less than 16, so one of these must be assigned in the last position in the optimal sequence. J_2 is selected since $p_2 > p_1$. Excluding J_2, the sum of the remaining processing times is 12. Jobs J_1 and J_5 are candidates of position 5; job J_5 is selected since $p_5 > p_2$. Continuing in this way, a sequence is obtained as $J_3 - J_1 - J_4 - J_5 - J_2$. For this sequence, the mean flow time is 7.6 while for the former EDD schedule $\bar{F} = 9.0$

7.3 Single-Stage Group Production Scheduling

7.3.1 Group Production Scheduling Model

As stated in the introduction, it is expected that in addition to the benefits from the pure-production technological viewpoints attained by group technology, an additional benefit is achieved by applying this philosophy to the production scheduling. In processing a large variety of jobs, several results such as possibility of flow pattern, reduction of setup time, learning effects, and reduction of the fraction defective, will be obtained by processing the jobs with the same or similar operations in succession.

Based on the above consideration, in this section production scheduling models of a new type have been developed for the purpose of improving the productivity in small- and medium-sized lot manufacturing based on the concept of group technology. In the scheduling models, jobs having the same or similar operations are assumed to be classified into the same group and associated with the concept of group technology is referred to as "group production scheduling" or "group scheduling" for short.

The fundamental assumptions of the group scheduling models are as follows [5,6]:

1. Jobs to be processed are classified into several groups and jobs within the same group are processed in succession.
2. Group processing time required for completion of a group consists of group setup time and the sum of processing times contained for jobs in each group.
3. Group setup time needed to process a group is independent of the sequence of groups.
4. Job setup time needed to process a job is independent of the sequences of groups and jobs and it is included in the job processing time.
5. In the case of a multistage production system, all jobs and groups are processed in a flow-shop pattern. (All jobs and groups follow the same path from one stage to another.) Furthermore, the ordering of groups and jobs is assumed to be the same on each machine. (No passing of groups and jobs is allowed.)

Table 7.2 shows the group scheduling where jobs are classified into N groups, each of which consists of n_i jobs ($i = 1, 2, \ldots, N$).

In the group scheduling models defined above, there are $N! \times \Pi_{i=1}^{N} n_i!$ feasible schedules on each machine. On the other hand, in many conventional scheduling problems where there exists no precedence relation among jobs, the number of sequences to be evaluated is $n!$ on each machine in the case of n jobs. Therefore, the conventional scheduling can be regarded as a kind of group scheduling in which only one group consisting of n jobs is involved or each of N groups contains only one job.

In the group scheduling problem, optimal decisions are to be made as to the sequence of groups classified and the sequence of jobs in each group. In this book, they are called "group sequence" and "job sequence," respectively. Furthermore, a schedule in which both group and job sequences are specified is called a "group schedule."

There is a string problem that seems to be similar to the group scheduling problem. However, significant differences exist between both problems in that the string problem has no background of group technology, considers only the sequence of groups classified excluding the sequence of jobs in each group, and does not include group setup times in its model.

Table 7.2. Group Scheduling under Static Conditions

Group	G_1			G_2			$\ldots$	G_N		
Job	J_{11}	J_{12}	$\ldots$ J_{1n_1}	J_{21}	J_{22}	$\ldots$ J_{2n_2}	$\ldots$	J_{N1}	J_{N2}	$\ldots$ J_{Nn_N}

In the string problem, theoretical analyses have been made as to the single-machine problems of minimizing certain measures of performance and the two-machine flow-shop problems [7] of minimizing the makespan. However, there have been only a few studies treating both sequences of groups and jobs simultaneously. In this section and in the next chapter, analyses of the group scheduling problems under static conditions are performed and several effective theorems and algorithms for determining optimal group schedules are developed.

This section treats a single-machine group scheduling problem that is the most basic one in group production scheduling. The scheduling criteria employed in this section are the minimum mean flow time and minimum weighted flow time. The problem is to determine an optimal group schedule (optimal sequence of groups and optimal sequences of jobs in groups) minimizing each of the above performance measures.

It is supposed that jobs to be processed are classified into N groups, each of which consists of n_i jobs ($i = 1, 2, \ldots, N$). Let $J_{i\xi}$ ($i = 1, 2, \ldots, N, \xi = 1, 2, \ldots, n_i$) denote the jth job in group G_i ($i = 1, 2, \ldots, N$) and $p_{i\xi}$ denote the job processing time including job setup time. Furthermore, let S_i ($i = 1, 2, \ldots, N$) denote the group setup time of group G_i.

In the scheduling problem defined, the makespan is no longer a suitable one as in the case of the conventional scheduling problem. The makespan is given by:

$$F_{\max} = \sum_{i=1}^{N} S_i + \sum_{i=1}^{N} \sum_{\xi=1}^{n_i} p_{i\xi} \qquad (7.15)$$

Hence, the makespan is not dependent on the order of groups and jobs for a single-machine group scheduling problem.

7.3.2 Minimizing Mean Flow Time and Weighted Mean Flow Time

The criteria of the minimum mean flow time and the minimum weighted mean flow time are tractable even in group scheduling. In this subsection, a theorem that gives the optimal group schedule minimizing the mean flow time is offered, [8] and then it is extended to the criterion of the minimum weighted mean flow time. The symbol ( ) is used to signify the order of groups or jobs in a group schedule.

The completion time of $J_{(i)(\xi)}$, the ξth job in the ith group, is:

$$C_{(i)(\xi)} = \sum_{u=1}^{i-1} (S_{(u)} + P_{(u)}) + S_{(i)} + \sum_{v=1}^{\xi} P_{(i)(v)} \qquad (7.16)$$

where $P_{(i)} = (\sum_{\xi=1}^{n(i)} P_{(i)(\xi)})$ is the total processing time of group $G_{(i)}$.

Since the ready times of all jobs are to be zero, the flow time of $J_{(i)(\xi)}$ is simply:

$$F_{(i)(\xi)} = C_{(i)(\xi)} \qquad (7.17)$$

Thus the mean flow time is obtained by:

$$\bar{F} = \sum_{i=1}^{N} \sum_{\xi=1}^{n(i)} F_{(i)(\xi)} / \sum_{i=1}^{N} n_i$$

$$= \frac{1}{M} \sum_{i=1}^{N} n_{(i)} \sum_{u=1}^{i-1} Q_{(u)} + \frac{1}{M} \sum_{i=1}^{N} n_{(i)} S_{(i)} + \frac{1}{M} \sum_{i=1}^{N} \sum_{\xi=1}^{n(i)} \sum_{v=1}^{\xi} P_{(i)(v)} \qquad (7.18)$$

where $Q_{(i)}(=S_{(i)} + P_{(i)})$ is the group processing time of $G_{(i)}$ and $M (=\sum_{i=1}^{N} n_i)$ is the number of all jobs.

In the above equation, the second term is a constant. The first term is concerned with the group sequence and is independent of the job sequences because $Q_{(i)}$ is a constant. The last term is concerned with the job sequence in each group, and is not influenced by the group sequence. Hence, the group sequence and the job sequences can be determined independently of each other.

The first term is minimized by ordering the groups in nondecreasing order of Q_i/n_i. The last one is minimized by ordering the jobs in nondecreasing order of job processing times for each group. Thus the results are stated formally as a theorem.

Theorem 7.4. In a single-machine group scheduling problem, the mean flow time is minimized by ordering the jobs in each group and between the groups such that

$$P_{(i)(1)} \le P_{(i)(2)} \le \ldots \le P_{(i)(n_i)} \ (i = 1, 2, \ldots, N)$$

and

$$\frac{S_{(1)} + P_{(1)}}{n_{(1)}} \le \frac{S_{(2)} + P_{(2)}}{n_{(2)}} \le \ldots \le \frac{S_{(N)} + P_{(N)}}{n_{(N)}} \qquad (7.19)$$

Strictly speaking, $p_{(i)(n_i)}$ in the above equation should be expressed as $p_{(i)(n_{(i)})}$ in the context. However, the expression $P_{(i)(n_i)}$ is used here for simplicity.

In some cases, jobs do not have equal importance. A value or weighting factor, $w_{i\xi}$ ($i = 1, 2, \ldots, N, \xi = 1, 2, \ldots, n_i$) is assumed to be given for each job to describe its relative importance.

The weighted mean flow time is given by the following equation, similar to equation 7.18.

$$\bar{F}_w = \frac{1}{M} \sum_{i=1}^{N} \sum_{\xi=1}^{n(i)} w_{(i)(\xi)} \sum_{j=1}^{i-1} Q_{(j)} + \frac{1}{M} \sum_{i=1}^{N} \sum_{\xi=1}^{n(i)} w_{(i)(\xi)} S_{(i)}$$

$$+ \frac{1}{M} \sum_{i=1}^{N} \sum_{\xi=1}^{n(i)} \sum_{v=1}^{\xi} w_{(i)(v)} p_{(i)(v)} \qquad (7.20)$$

In the case of minimizing the weighted mean flow time, the following theorem, which is an extension of theorem 7.4, holds.

Theorem 7.5. In a single-machine group scheduling problem, the weighted mean flow time is minimized by ordering the jobs in each group and the groups respectively, such that

$$\frac{p_{(i)(1)}}{w_{(i)(1)}} \le \frac{p_{(i)(2)}}{w_{(i)(2)}} \le \ldots \le \frac{p_{(i)(n_i)}}{w_{(i)(n_i)}} \quad (i = 1, 2, \ldots, N)$$

and

$$\frac{S_{(1)} + P_{(1)}}{\sum_{\xi=1}^{n(1)} w_{(1)(\xi)}} \le \frac{S_{(2)} + P_{(2)}}{\sum_{\xi=1}^{n(2)} w_{(2)(\xi)}} \le \ldots \le \frac{S_{(N)} + P_{(N)}}{\sum_{\xi=1}^{n(N)} w_{(N)(\xi)}} \qquad (7.21)$$

Example 7.2. Consider a three-group, eight-job, single-machine group scheduling problem as shown in table 7.3. In this case, the makespan is the sum of the job processing times for all jobs and constant as follows:

$$F_{max} = (2 + 4 + 3) + (3 + 6 + 2 + 5) + (1 + 5 + 4 + 3) = 38$$

According to theorem 7.4, under the criterion of minimizing the mean flow time, the optimal job sequences and the optimal group sequence are obtained by ordering the jobs in each group and the groups, respectively. Hence, job sequence for each group is $J_{12} - J_{11}$, $J_{22} - J_{23} - J_{21}$, and $J_{33} - J_{32} - J_{31}$, respectively. The group processing time for each group is 9, 16, and 13, respectively; hence, the group sequence is $G_1 - G_3 - G_2$. Accordingly, the optimal group schedule is determined as $G_1(J_{12} - J_{11}) - G_3(J_{33} - J_{32} -$

Table 7.3.   Basic Data for a Three-Group, Eight-Job Group Scheduling Problem

Group	G_1		G_2			G_3		
Job	J_{11}	J_{12}	J_{21}	J_{22}	J_{23}	J_{31}	J_{32}	J_{33}
Job processing time	4	3	6	2	5	5	4	3
Weight	2	1	2	1	3	2	1	1
Group setup time		2		3			1		

$J_{31}) - G_2(J_{22} - J_{23} - J_{21})$. The Gantt chart of this group schedule is represented in figure 7.1. The mean flow time for jobs is calculated as follows:

$$\bar{F} = [(F_{12} + F_{11}) + (F_{33} + F_{32} + F_{31}) + (F_{22} + F_{23} + F_{21})]/8$$
$$= [(5 + 9) + (13 + 17 + 22) + (27 + 32 + 38)]/8$$
$$= 20.4$$

On the other hand, the optimal group schedule minimizing the weighted mean flow time is obtained by sequencing the jobs in each group and between groups in order of nondecreasing $p_{(i)(\xi)}/w_{(i)(\xi)}$ and $Q_{(i)}/\sum_{\xi=1}^{n(i)} w_{(i)(\xi)}$, respectively. Hence, from table 7.4 the optimal group schedule is determined as $G_2(J_{23} - J_{22} - J_{21}) - G_1(J_{11} - J_{12}) - G_3(J_{31} - J_{33} - J_{32})$.

The weighted mean flow time of this schedule is

$$\bar{F}_w = [(w_{23}F_{23} + w_{22}F_{22} + w_{21}F_{21}) + (w_{11}F_{11} + w_{12}F_{12})$$
$$+ (w_{31}F_{31} + w_{33}F_{33} + w_{32}F_{32})]/8$$
$$= [(3 \times 8 + 1 \times 10 + 2 \times 16) + (2 \times 22 + 1 \times 25)$$
$$+ (2 \times 31 + 1 \times 34 + 1 \times 38)]/8$$
$$= 33.6$$

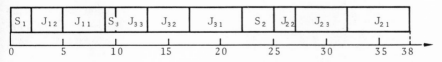

Figure 7.1.   The Gantt chart of the schedule minimizing the mean flow time

Table 7.4. List of $p_{i\xi}/w_{i\xi}$ and $Q_i/\Sigma_{\xi=1}^{n_j} w_{i\xi}$

Group	G_1		G_2			G_3		
Job	J_{11}	J_{12}	J_{21}	J_{22}	J_{23}	J_{31}	J_{32}	J_{33}
$p_{i\xi}/w_{i\xi}$	$2^{(1)}$	3	3	2	5/3	5/2	4	3
$Q_i/\sum_{\xi=1}^{n_i} w_{i\xi}$	$3^{(2)}$		8/3			13/4		

Note: (1) = 4 ÷ 2; (2) = (2 + 4 + 3)/(2 + 1) = 3.

The criterion concerning jobs' due date, especially the minimum total tardiness, is important in production scheduling. However, even the single-machine scheduling problem of minimizing the total tardiness is known as NP complete. Hence, none of the complete solution procedures have been presented. But Emmons gave several theorems that establish the relative order of pairs of jobs and proposed a relatively efficient implicit algorithm [9]. An extension of his theory to group scheduling has been made and algorithms for determining an optimal and near-optimal group schedule have been developed [5].

References

1. Conway, R. W., Maxwell, W. L., and Miller, L. W. *Theory of Scheduling.* Reading, Mass.: Addison-Wesley Publishing Co., 1967.
2. Baker, K. R. *Introduction to Sequencing and Scheduling.* New York: John Wiley and Sons, 1974.
3. Kan, A. H. G. R. *Machine Scheduling Problems—Classification, Complexity, and Computations.* The Hague: Martinus Nijhoff, 1976.
4. Little, J.D.C., Murty, K.G., Sweeny, D.W., and Karel, C. "An Algorithm for the Traveling Salesman Problem." *Operations Research,* 11, No. 6, pp. 972–983, 1963.
5. Yoshida, T., Nakamura, N., and Hitomi, K. "Group Production Scheduling for Minimum Total Tardiness." *AIIE Transactions,* 10(2), pp. 157–162, 1978.
6. Hitomi, K., and Ham, I. "Operation Scheduling for Group Technology Applications." *CIRP Annals,* 25 (August, 1976), pp. 419–422.
7. Kurisu, T. "Two-Machine Scheduling under Required Precedence among Jobs." *J. Opns. Res. Soc.* (Japan), 19(1), pp. 1–13, 1976.

8. Yoshida, T., Nakamura, N., and Hitomi, K. "A Study of Production Scheduling (Optimization of Group Scheduling on a Single Production Stage)." (Japanese), *Transactions of the Japan Society of Mechanical Engineers*, 39(322), pp. 1993–2003, 1973.
9. Emmons, H. "One-Machine Sequencing to Minimize Certain Functions of Job Tardiness." *Operations Research*, 17(4), pp. 701–715, 1969.

8 MULTI-STAGE GROUP PRODUCTION SCHEDULING

8.1 Flow-Shop Scheduling

Flow-shop scheduling problems are more difficult to solve as compared with sequencing problems, but these problems are relatively tractable as compared with job-shop scheduling problems. Several theoretical analyses have been made to solve the flow-shop scheduling problems.

The first step of development for the flow-shop scheduling theory dates back to Johnson's work in 1954 for the two-stage (two-machine) flow-shop scheduling problem of minimizing the makespan [1]. Johnson gave a theorem that establishes the relative order in which pairs of jobs are processed in an optimal schedule and developed a working rule (algorithm) with which an optimal schedule can be easily constructed.

In general, flow-shop scheduling problems including three machines or more are said to be NP complete; therefore, no simple rule has been offered for determining the optimal schedule.

However, Johnson showed in his original representation that a generalization of his theorem to the three-machine flow-shop case is possible when the second machine is dominated by the first or second machine. Moreover, several researchers solved the K-machine special structure flow-shop scheduling problems, where processing times were not completely random but bore a well-defined relationship to one another. Theories of flow-shop scheduling problems are mainly concerned with the criterion of the minimum makespan, and they have been developed based upon Johnson's theorem. For other criteria, the K-machine flow-shop scheduling problems have not yet been solved theoretically.

In solving flow-shop scheduling problems, the following two properties that prescribe the same job order on initial and terminal machines are useful.

Theorem 8.1. For the flow-shop scheduling problems of minimizing any regular measure of performance, it is sufficient to consider only schedules in which the same order of jobs is prescribed on the first two machines.

Theorem 8.2. For the flow-shop scheduling problems of minimizing the makespan, it is sufficient to consider only schedules in which the same order is prescribed on the first two machines and the same order is also prescribed on the last two machines.

Therefore, for the flow-shop scheduling problems of four or more machines, a general type of schedule that has different orders of jobs on each machine must be considered to find an optimal schedule in the true sense of the word. However, for simplicity of analysis, it is assumed that the processing order of jobs is the same on each machine (no passing of jobs is allowed).

Consider a K-machine flow-shop scheduling problem of minimizing the makespan. In order to express the makespan by using the processing times for jobs on each machine, develop the recursive relation of the completion time on machine M_k of $J_{(i)}$, which indicates the ith job in a schedule.

In the flow-shop scheduling, the completion time of $J_{(i)}$ on M_k is given by (see figure 8.1):

$$C_{(i)}^k = \max(C_{(i)}^{k-1}, C_{(i-1)}^k) + p_{(i)}^k \qquad (8.1)$$

where

$$C_{(i)}^0 = C_{(0)}^k = 0.$$

First, by using this recursive relation repeatedly, the makespan for the two-machine flow-shop scheduling problem; that is, the completion time on M_2 of $J_{(n)}$, is expressed as

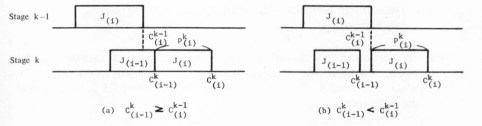

Figure 8.1. Completion time of job on kth machine

$$F_{\max} = C^2_{(n)} = \max_{1 \leq u \leq n} \left(\sum_{i=1}^{u} p^1_{(i)} + \sum_{i=u}^{n} p^2_{(i)} \right) \qquad (8.2)$$

Extending this result to the K-machine flow-shop scheduling problem, we have

$$F_{\max} = C^K_{(n)} = \max_{1 \leq u_1 \leq u_2 \leq \cdots \leq u_{K-1} \leq n} \left(\sum_{i=1}^{u_1} p^1_{(i)} + \sum_{i=u_1}^{u_2} p^2_{(i)} + \cdots + \sum_{i=u_{K-1}}^{n} p^K_{(i)} \right)$$

$$(8.3)$$

The problem is to determine a sequence so as to minimize the above equation.

Furthermore, we can develop another expression of the makespan by using the idle times of jobs on the last stage, which is helpful to estimate the lower bound for the makespan. The completion time, $C^k_{(i)}$, given by equation 8.1 is also denoted as:

$$C^k_{(i)} = \sum_{j=1}^{i} (g^k_{(j)} + p^k_{(j)}) \qquad (8.4)$$

where $g_{(j)}$ is the idle time of M_k before processing $J_{(j)}$ after completion of $J_{(j-1)}$, and is given by:

$$g^k_{(j)} = \begin{cases} C^{k-1}_{(j)} - C^k_{(j-1)}, & \text{if } C^{k-1}_{(j)} > C^k_{(j-1)} \\ 0, & \text{otherwise} \end{cases}$$

As a result, the makespan is given by:

$$F_{\max} = C^K_{(n)} = \sum_{i=1}^{n} (g^K_{(i)} + p^K_{(i)}) \qquad (8.5)$$

8.1.1 Two-Stage Scheduling Problem of Minimizing the Makespan

For the two-machine flow-shop scheduling problem of minimizing the makespan, it is clear from theorem 8.1 that it is sufficient to consider only permutation schedules. The makespan given by equation 8.1 is transformed into the following:

$$F_{\max} = \max_{1 \leq u \leq n} \left(\sum_{i=1}^{u} p_{(i)}^{1} - \sum_{i=1}^{u-1} p_{(i)}^{2} \right) + \sum_{i=1}^{n} p_{(i)}^{2} \qquad (8.6)$$

In the above equation, the second term is constant. Therefore, minimizing the makespan is equivalent to minimizing the first term, which induces the following well-known theorem.

Theorem 8.3 [Johnson's theorem].   An optimal ordering is given by the following rule:

Job J_i precedes Job J_j if

$$\min(p_i^1, p_j^2) < \min(p_j^1, p_i^2) \qquad (8.7)$$

If there is equality, either ordering is optimal.

Based on this theorem, Johnson constructed the following working rule for determining an optimal schedule.

Johnson's algorithm for minimizing the makespan for the two-machine flow-shop scheduling problem.

Step 1. Find the minimum value among the values of p_i^1's and p_i^2's under consideration. (IN the case of a tie, select arbitrarily.)

Step 2. If it is p_a^1, place J_a first, and if it is p_a^2, place J_a last.

Step 3. Remove the assigned job from consideration and go back to step 1.

Example 8.1. Consider a five-job, two-machine flow-shop scheduling problem of minimizing the makespan, as shown in table 8.1.

An optimal schedule is determined by Johnson's algorithm as follows: The minimum value is 1, which is the processing time of J_3 on M_1; J_3 is placed first in an optimal schedule. Remove this job from consideration. The minimum value among the remaining four jobs is two, the processing time of J_1 on M_2; as a result, J_1 is placed in the last position. Remove this job from consideration. Proceeding in the same manner, an optimal schedule is

Table 8.1. Basic data for a five-job, two-machine flow-shop scheduling problem

Job	J_1	J_2	J_3	J_4	J_5
Processing time on machine M_1	5	6	1	9	3
Processing time on machine M_2	2	3	4	5	7

determined as $J_3 - J_5 - J_4 - J_2 - J_1$. The makespan for this schedule is easily obtained by depicting the Gantt chart, as indicated in figure 8.2; that is, $F_{max} = 26$.

For the two-machine flow-shop scheduling problem of minimizing the makespan, several researchers considered the problem with time lags between the production of a job on the first machine and its production on the second one and gave decision rules that are extensions of Johnson's theorem [2].

In general, when workpieces (parts) are processed on machines, setup times are needed to set up the machines for the processing of their operations. In Johnson-type problems, however, no attention has been directed to the setup times; that is, the setup times are assumed to be independent of the sequence and to be included in the processing times. In many actual cases, setup for a job and its processing happens to be independent of each other. Therefore, setup for an operation of a job on a preceding machine can be done before completion of the operation of the job on the succeeding machine. In such a situation, it is not valid to absorb the setup time in the processing time. Therefore, from the standpoint of actual production scheduling, decisions should be made by separating the setup times from the processing times.

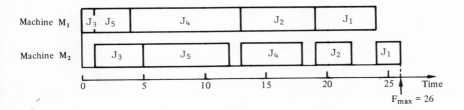

Figure 8.2. Gantt chart for the optimal schedule minimizing the makespan

8.1.2 Scheduling Problem with Setup Times Separated

It is the purpose of this subsection to describe a scheduling model with setup times separated [3]. For constructing this new type scheduling model, it is assumed that setup for an operation of a job on machine M_2 can be done before completion of the operation of the job on machine M_1 if there exist some idle times on machine M_2 (see figure 8.3). In the model, the time required to complete each job on each machine consists of job setup time and job processing time, each of which is a scheduling unit. Let setup time and processing time for job J_i on machine M_k be denoted by s_i^k and p_i^k, respectively.

First, examine whether the property that the same order on the first two machines and the last two machines will be sure to give an optimal schedule for the K-stage (K-machine) flow-shop scheduling that is applicable to the problem with setup times separated. Even for the scheduling problem with setup times separated, the following theorem holds.

Theorem 8.4. For the flow-shop scheduling problem with setup times separated, it is sufficient to consider only schedules in which the same order occurs on the first two machines when the objective is to minimize the makespan.

This theorem can be easily proven with an argument which resembles that given for the problem with setup times included. It is worth noting that the separation of setup times from processing times makes it unnecessary for an optimal schedule to have the same order on the last two machines. A simple example will illustrate this. Suppose that two jobs are to be scheduled on a three-machine flow-shop to minimize the makespan. The production data of the two jobs are shown in table 8.2. There are two schedules, S_1 and S_2, that have the same order on machine M_2 and M_3. The makespan of the two schedules are 16 and 17 hours, respectively. However, there is a schedule S_3

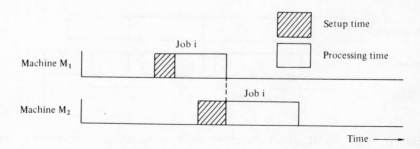

Figure 8.3. Independence of setup and processing [3]

Table 8.2. Production data for three-machine scheduling in hours [3]

Job	I		J	
Setup time/processing time	s_1^k	p_1^k	s_2^k	p_2^k
Machine M_1	1	3	1	1
Machine M_2	1	1	2	5
Machine M_3	5	1	1	4

with different orderings on machines M_2 and M_3 with the makespan of 15 hours (see figure 8.4).

In the case of the two-machine flow-shop scheduling problem with setup times separated, the optimal schedule minimizing the makespan can be characterized by the following rule for ordering pairs of jobs.

Theorem 8.5. For the two-stage flow-shop scheduling problem with setup times separated, an optimal schedule under the criterion of the minimum makespan is given by the following rule:

Job J_i precedes J_j if

$$\min(s_i^1 - s_i^2 + p_i^1, p_j^2) < \min(s_j^1 - s_j^2 + p_j^1, p_i^2) \qquad (8.8)$$

If there is equality, either ordering is optimal.

This theorem is an extension of Johnson's, since by letting setup times be zero, inequality (equation 8.8) becomes exactly the one Johnson gave in his paper. With adaptation of this theorem, an optimal schedule is directly constructed by the following algorithm which is similar to Johnson's algorithm.

Optimizing algorithm for the 2-machine flow-shop scheduling with setup times separated.

Step 1. Find the minimum value of $(s_i^1 - s_i^2 + p_i^1)$ and p_i^2 $(i = 1, 2, \ldots, n)$ under consideration. (In the case of a tie, select arbitrarily.)

Step 2. If it is $(s_a^1 - s_a^2 + p_a^1)$, place J_a first, and if it is p_a^2, place J_a last.

Step 3. Remove the assigned job from consideration and go back to step 1.

Example 8.2. Consider a four-job scheduling problem which has production data as shown in table 8.3. First, calculating the values of $r_i^1(=s_i^1 - s_i^2 + p_i^1)$ and $r_i^2(=p_i^2)$, we obtain $[(r_1^1, r_1^2), (r_2^1, r_2^2), (r_3^1, r_3^2), (r_4^1, r_4^2)] = [(9, 8), (4,$

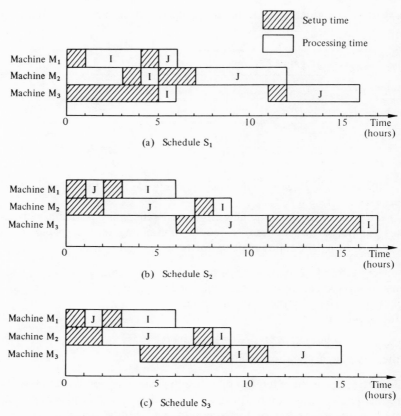

Figure 8.4. Schedules on three machines [3]

7), (8, 3) (10, 9)]. By using the algorithm proposed in the above, an optimal schedule is determined as $J_2 - J_4 - J_1 - J_3$ with the makespan of 41 hours.

In order to clarify the effect of the setup time consideration on the reduction of the makespan, find an optimal schedule with setup times included. In this case, the processing times including the setup times are given by $[\{(s_1^1 + p_1^1), (s_1^2 + p_1^2)\}, \{(s_2^1 + p_2^1),(s_2^2 + p_2^2)\}, \{(s_3^1 + p_3^1), \quad (s_3^2 + p_3^2)\}, \{(s_4^1 + p_4^1), (s_4^2 + p_4^2)\}] = [(12, 11), (6, 9), (9, 4), (11, 10)]$; hence, by using Johnson's algorithm, the optimal schedule is obtained as $J_2 - J_1 - J_4 - J_3$ with the makespan of 43 hours. Accordingly, the amount of the time reduction due to the setup time consideration is 2 hours for this example. The Gantt charts of the two schedules are shown in figure 8.5.

Table 8.3. Production data for two-machine scheduling in hours. [3]

Job	J_1		J_2		J_3		J_4	
Setup time/processing time	s_1^k	p_1^k	s_2^k	p_2^k	s_3^k	p_3^k	s_4^k	p_4^k
Machine M_1	2	10	1	5	2	7	3	8
Machine M_2	3	8	2	7	1	3	1	9

8.1.3 Large-Scale Flow-Shop Scheduling Problem

In general, K-stage ($K \geq 3$) flow-shop scheduling problems are known to be NP complete even for the most simple scheduling criterion of minimizing the makespan. Therefore, no simple rule for determining optimal schedules with less computational efforts has been offered for the large-scale scheduling problems. Thus general purpose methodologies for solving combinatorial problems, such as dynamic programming and branch-and-bound methods, have been applied to solve the problems. By using these methods, problems of small or medium size can be solved with relatively fewer computational efforts, although large-size problems require much more computational efforts.

Theoretical approach. Several researchers have investigated the K-stage flow-shop scheduling problems ($K \geq 3$). The first step of these works was found in Johnson's work, in which he showed that a generalization of his theorem to the three-machine case is possible when the second machine is dominated. Later, Johnson's results are more generalized to the K-stage flow-shop scheduling problems where the processing times are not completely random but bear a well-defined relationship to one another [4, 5, 6]. The proposed algorithms for determining optimal schedules are all simple and computationally efficient and can solve large-scale problems even with manual computational devices, as in the case of Johnson's algorithm.

If each of the following well-defined relationships holds among job processing times at each of the stages, the K-stage flow-shop scheduling problem can be reduced to the two-stage one, and therefore, is solved easily by using Johnson's theorem.

Case 1. For a fixed $h < K - 1$, the processing times satisfy the following conditions:

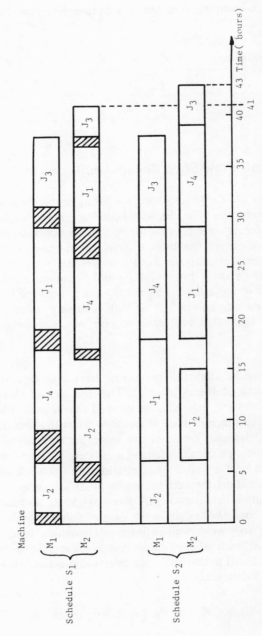

Figure 8.5. The Gantt charts of schedule S_1 with setup times separated and schedule S_2 with setup times included

(i) $\quad \min_{1\le i\le n} p_i^k \ge \max_{1\le i\le n} p_i^{k+1} \qquad \forall k \le h-1 \le K-2$

(ii) $\quad \max_{1\le i\le n} p_i^k \le \min_{1\le i\le n} p_i^{k+1} \qquad \forall h+1 \le k \le K-1$ $\qquad (8.9)$

When $K=2$, none of the above conditions is required since the possible value of h is 1. However, when $K=3$, one of the following conditions which are Johnson's special three-machine case holds:

$$\left. \begin{array}{c} \min\limits_{1\le i\le n} p_i^1 \ge \max\limits_{1\le i\le n} p_i^2 \\[2mm] \max\limits_{1\le i\le n} p_i^2 \le \min\limits_{1\le i\le n} p_i^3 \end{array} \right\} \qquad (8.10)$$

Hence, case 1 is just the extension of Johnson's special three-machine case to a special K-machine (K-stage) case.

Case 2. The processing times satisfy the following conditions:

$$\max_{1\le i\le n} p_i^k \le \min_{1\le i\le n} p_i^{k+1} \qquad \forall k \le K-2 \qquad (8.11)$$

Case 3. The processing times satisfy the following conditions:

$$\max_{1\le i\le n} p_i^{k+1} \le \min_{1\le i\le n} p_i^k \qquad \forall 2 \le k \le K-1 \qquad (8.12)$$

For case 1, the makespan given by equation 8.3 is transformed into the following:

$$F_{\max} = \max_{1\le u\le n} \left(\sum_{i=1}^{u}\sum_{k=1}^{K-1} p_{(i)}^k - \sum_{i=1}^{u-1}\sum_{k=2}^{K} p_{(i)}^k \right) + \sum_{i=1}^{n} p_{(i)}^K \qquad (8.13)$$

This expression has the same form as equation 8.6 for the two-stage flow-shop scheduling problem. Therefore, the following theorem is obtained for case 1.

Theorem 8.6. If the processing times satisfy condition 8.9, an optimal schedule is obtained by the following rule:
  Job J_i precedes job J_j if

$$\min \left(\sum_{k=1}^{K-1} p_i^k, \sum_{k=2}^{K} p_j^k \right) < \min \left(\sum_{k=1}^{K-1} p_j^k, \sum_{k=2}^{K} p_i^k \right) \qquad (8.14)$$

If there is equality, either ordering is optimal.

With the help of this theorem, an optimal schedule can be easily determined by the following algorithm.

Optimizing algorithm for case 1.

Step 1. Calculate the fictitious processing times, the values of $X_i = \sum_{k=1}^{K-1} p_i^k$, $Y_i = \sum_{k=2}^{K} p_i^k$ for each job.
Step 2. Determine an optimal schedule by applying Johnson's algorithm to these values.

Example 8.3. Consider a five-job, four-machine flow-shop scheduling problem as shown in table 8.4. The processing times satisfy condition 8.9 for $h = 1$ as follows:

$$\max_{1 \le i \le 5} p_i^2 (=7) \le \min_{1 \le i \le 5} p_i^3 (=7)$$

$$\max_{1 \le i \le 5} p_i^3 (=10) \le \min_{1 \le i \le 5} p_i^4 (=11)$$

Thus the optimal sequence minimizing the makespan is determined by using the optimizing algorithm. The values of X_i and Y_i for each job are calculated as $[(X_1, Y_1), (X_2, Y_2), (X_3, Y_3), (X_4, Y_4), (X_5, Y_5)] = [(30, 29), (19, 27), (25, 23), (21, 29), (28, 24)]$. (For example, $X_1 = \sum_{k=1}^{3} p_1^k = 13 + 7 + 10 = 30$ and $Y_1 = \sum_{k=2}^{4} p_1^k = 7 + 10 + 12 = 29$).

By applying Johnson's algorithm to this list, the optimal schedule is determined as $J_2 - J_4 - J_1 - J_5 - J_3$ with the makespan of 81. The Gantt chart of this schedule is shown in figure 8.6.

Table 8.4. Processing times for a five-job, four-machine flow-shop scheduling

Stage \ Job	J_1	J_2	J_3	J_4	J_5
M_1	13	7	13	5	15
M_2	7	5	4	7	6
M_3	10	7	8	9	7
M_4	12	15	11	13	11

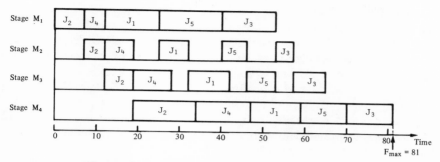

Figure 8.6. Gantt chart for the optimal schedule

When the processing times satisfy the condition for case 2, the makespan is expressed as

$$F_{max} = \sum_{k=1}^{K-2} p_{(1)}^k + \max_{1 \le u_{K-1} \le n} \left(\sum_{i=1}^{u_{K-1}} p_{(i)}^{K-1} - \sum_{i=1}^{u_{K-1}-1} p_{(i)}^K \right) + \sum_{i=1}^{n} p_{(i)}^K \quad (8.15)$$

A sequence minimizing the above equation is determined by the following algorithm.

Optimizing algorithm for case 2.

Step 1. Determine an optimal sequence S for the two-stage problem (stages M_{K-1} and M_K). Let J_a be the first job of schedule S.
Step 2. Find $\Pi = \{i_j \,|\, \Sigma_{k=1}^{K-2} p_{ij}^k < \Sigma_{k=1}^{K-2} p_a^k\}$ ($j = 1, 2, \ldots, l$). Generate l new schedules by assigning each job $J_i \in \Pi$ to the first position and maintaining the order of schedule S for the remaining jobs.
Step 3. Among the $(l + 1)$ schedules obtained above, including schedule S, find the schedule minimizing the makespan. This schedule is optimal.

For case 3, an algorithm similar to the one above can be developed for determining an optimal schedule.

Branch-and-Bound approach.   In the previous subsection, the special structure flow-shop scheduling problems were theoretically solved. However, for solving general flow-shop scheduling problems, we must rely on the general-purpose methodologies such as dynamic programming and the branch-and-bound method, although these methods usually require many computational efforts to find an optimal solution for large-sized problems.

Above all, the branch-and-bound method is the most widely used solution method for optimally solving the flow-shop scheduling problems.

With some success, the branch-and-bound method has been employed to solve several scheduling problems. The application of this method to the traveling salesman problem was successfully made by Little et al. [7].

Now apply this method to the flow-shop scheduling problem of minimizing the makespan, which was a method basically developed by Ignall and Schrage [8] and independently by Lomnicki [9]. As stated in chapter 5, the branch-and-bound method consists of two fundamental procedures: branching and bounding procedures. The two fundamental procedures of the method follow.

The branching procedure. The set of permutations of job indices is partitioned into several subsets. By this procedure, nodes, each of which represents a subset of the sequence of jobs, are repeatedly created. Let N_s be a node at which the sequence of s jobs is determined: $N_s = [J_{(1)}, J_{(2)}, \ldots, J_{(s)}]$. Branching from this node consists of taking each of $(n - s)$ unallocated jobs and placing it in the sequence determined. Then new $(n - s)$ nodes, N_{s+1}, which have the sequence of $J_{(1)} - J_{(2)} - \ldots - J_{(s)} - J_{(s+1)}$ are created. Hence, a solution for the scheduling problem is obtained at node N_n in which the sequence of n jobs considered are specified. The problem remaining in the branching procedure is how to select a node to be branched among nodes created. Usually, a node having the largest lower bound is selected for branching in the case of a minimization problem.

The bounding procedure. The bounding procedure, which is another fundamental procedure, is that of calculating a lower bound on the solution to each subproblem generated in the branching process. The procedure for solving the problem treated calculates a lower bound on the makespan to each generated node representing a subset of the sequence of jobs.

A variety of lower bounds on the makespan have been developed for the flow-shop scheduling problems. Representative of these bounds are the machine-based, the job-based, and the composite bound. The machine-based lower bound, which is the most basic one, is estimated at node N_s as follows:

$$LB(Ns) = \max_{1 \leq k \leq K} \left(C_{(s)}^k + \sum_{i \in \bar{J}} p_{(i)}^k + \min_{i \in \bar{J}} \sum_{h=k+1}^{K} p_{(i)}^h \right) \qquad (8.16)$$

where $C_{(s)}^k$ is the completion time of $J_{(s)}$ on M_k, and $\bar{J}$ is the set of the remaining $(n - s)$ jobs not yet sequenced.

The first term in the above equation is the total completion time on M_k for the s jobs already sequenced. The second term is the sum of processing times for the jobs not yet specified in the node. The last one represents the minimum of the sums of processing times on the remaining stages for each of the jobs not yet sequenced. Therefore, the machine-based lower bound at node N_s can be well estimated as a maximum from among the sums of these terms for all stages.

The above consideration leads to the following branch-and-bound algorithm for determining an optimal sequence to the flow-shop scheduling problem of minimizing the makespan.

Branch-and-bound algorithm for the minimum makespan flow-shop scheduling problem.

Step 1. Let the level of the node $s = 0$ and the least feasible value $L^* = \infty$.

Step 2. Branch the node N_s into $(n - s)$ nodes N_{s+1} by placing each of the jobs not yet allocated next in the sequence determined. Set $s = s + 1$.

Step 3. Calculate the lower bound $LB(N_s)$ for each of the new nodes.

Step 4. Find the job node having min $LB(N_s)$ from among the only job nodes newly created in the immediate previous branching in case of $L^* = \infty$, or from among all job nodes being active in case of $L^* \neq \infty$. (In the case of a tie, select the node with the largest value of s. Break the tie arbitrarily for the same s.) Let the level of the node selected by s and $LB^*(N_s) = $ min $LB(N_s)$.

Step 5. If $LB(N_s) \geq L^*$, stop. (The job sequence of the node having L^* is optimal.) Otherwise, go to step 6.

Step 6. If $s < n$, then go back to step 2. Otherwise, set $L^* = LB^*(N_s)$, and go back to step 4.

Example 8.4. Consider a four-job, five-machine flow-shop scheduling problem of minimizing the makespan, as shown in table 8.5. An optimal schedule is determined by using the branch-and-bound algorithm. The branching tree for this problem is represented in figure 8.7. The two figures just above and below each node indicate the node number and the machine-based lower bound on the makespan, respectively.

To begin with, set $s = 0$ and $L^* = \infty$(step 1). Four nodes are created from node N_0(all): $N_1 = [J_1]$, $[J_2]$, $[J_3]$, and $[J_4]$, and $s = 1$ (step 2). The lower bounds for all these nodes are calculated and indicated just above the nodes in figure 8.7. The detailed procedure for calculating the lower bound on node $[J_1]$ is shown by the following: First, for $C_{(1)}^k$,

Table 8.5. Processing times for a four-job, five-machine flow-shop scheduling problem

| | | Stage | | | |
Job	M_1	M_2	M_3	M_4	M_5
J_1	5	3	12	4	7
J_2	9	12	15	6	11
J_3	10	9	5	12	8
J_4	7	8	10	9	13

$$C_{(1)}^1 = p_{(1)}^1 = 5$$
$$C_{(1)}^2 = p_{(1)}^1 + p_{(1)}^2 = 5 + 3 = 8$$
$$C_{(1)}^3 = p_{(1)}^1 + p_{(1)}^2 + p_{(1)}^3 = 5 + 3 + 12 = 20$$
$$C_{(1)}^4 = p_{(1)}^1 + p_{(1)}^2 + p_{(1)}^3 + p_{(1)}^4 = 5 + 3 + 12 + 4 = 24$$
$$C_{(1)}^5 = p_{(1)}^1 + p_{(1)}^2 + p_{(1)}^3 + p_{(1)}^4 + p_{(1)}^5 = 5 + 3 + 12 + 4 + 7 = 31$$

For $\sum_{i \in \bar{J}} p_i^k$ since $\bar{J}$ includes J_2, J_3, and J_4.

$$\sum_{i \in \bar{J}} p_i^1 = 9 + 10 + 7 = 26$$

$$\sum_{i \in \bar{J}} p_i^2 = 12 + 9 + 8 = 29$$

$$\sum_{i \in \bar{J}} p_i^3 = 15 + 5 + 10 = 30$$

$$\sum_{i \in \bar{J}} p_i^4 = 6 + 12 + 9 = 27$$

$$\sum_{i \in \bar{J}} p_i^5 = 11 + 8 + 13 = 32$$

For $\min_{i \in \bar{J}} \sum_{h=k+1}^{K} p_i^h \ (= q^k)$,

$$q^1 = \min(12 + 15 + 6 + 11, 9 + 5 + 12 + 8, 8 + 10 + 9 + 13)$$
$$= \min(44, 34, 40) = 34$$
$$q^2 = \min(15 + 6 + 11, 5 + 12 + 8, 10 + 9 + 13)$$
$$= \min(32, 25, 32) = 25$$

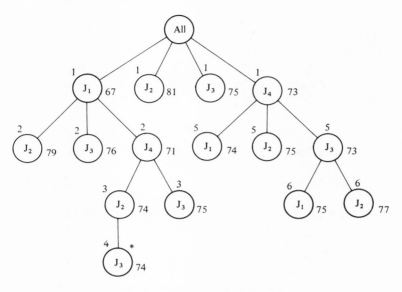

Figure 8.7. The branching tree for the four-job, five-machine flow-shop scheduling problem

$$q^3 = \min(6 + 11, 12 + 8, 9 + 13)$$

$$= \min(17, 20, 22) = 17$$

$$q^4 = \min(11, 8, 13) = 8$$

Hence, $LB(J_1) = \max(5 + 26 + 34, 8 + 29 + 25, 20 + 30 + 17, 24 + 27 + 8, 31 + 32) = \max(65, 62, 67, 59, 63) = 67$. Similarly, $LB(J_2) = 81$, $LB(J_3) = 75$, $LB(J_4) = 73$.

Then, proceeding to step 4, we choose the node with the lowest value of LB; in this case, node $[J_1]$ is selected. In step 5 since $LB(N_1) < L^*$, go back to step 6. Then in step 6 since $s(=1) < n(=4)$, go back to step 2. Three nodes $N_2 = [J_1 J_2]$, $[J_1 J_3]$, and $[J_1 J_4]$ are created from the node $[J_1]$. Then proceeding to step 3, the lower bounds are calculated in the same way as in the previous step 3. In step 4, we choose $[J_1 J_4]$, the node with the lowest lower bound, from among the three nodes since $L^* = \infty$.

Proceeding this way, at node $[J_1 J_4 J_2 J_3]$ with $LB = 74$, a feasible schedule is obtained; hence $L^* = 74$. However, there exists a node $[J_4]$ with the lower bound less than $L^* = 74$. From this node, new nodes are created and the lower bound for these nodes are calculated. There still exists a node

$[J_4 J_3]$ with $LB(= 73) < L^*(= 74)$. Branching is done from this node, resulting in two nodes $[J_4 J_3 J_1]$ with 75 and $[J_4 J_3 J_2]$ with 77. At this point, no node exists with the value of the lower bound less than L^* (= 74).

The optimal schedule is obtained as $J_1 - J_4 - J_2 - J_3$ at the node with L^*; the minimum makespan is 74 (min). The Gantt chart of this schedule is also shown in figure 8.8.

Heuristic Approach. The branch-and-bound method is one of the optimizing methods for combinatorial problems, and an optimal solution can always be found, while it requires great efforts to determine an optimal schedule for large-scale flow-shop scheduling problems. For such problems, it is better to get a near optimal schedule with less computational efforts than to get an optimal one with great computational ones. Such an approach is often called a "heuristic approach."

One heuristic method for the minimum makespan K-machine flow-shop scheduling problem is Petrov's method [10], which is an extension of Johnson's algorithm. The basic principle of the method consists of transforming a K-machine flow-shop scheduling problem into a two-machine flow-shop problem by dividing the matrix for job processing times into two parts. Petrov's algorithm is as follows:

Petrov's algorithm for the minimum makespan k-machine flow-shop scheduling problem.

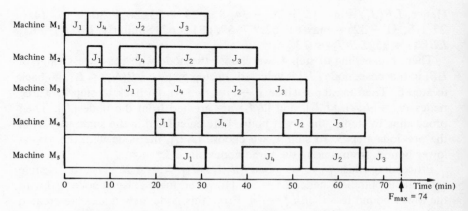

Figure 8.8.   Gantt chart for the optimal schedule

Step 1. Compute the following fictitious processing times:

$$P_i^A = \sum_{k=1}^{h} p_i^k$$

$$P_i^B = \sum_{k=h'}^{K} p_i^k$$

where $h = K/2$ and $h' = (K + 1)/2$ for even K and $h = h' = (K + 1)/2$ for odd K.

Step 2. Apply Johnson's algorithm to n jobs, each of which has the fictitious processing times.

Example 8.5. Determine a good schedule for a four-job, five-machine flow-shop scheduling problem of minimizing the makespan as shown in table 8.5, the same example as in the previous one. In this case $K = 5$, which is odd; hence $h = h' = (K + 1)/2 = 3$. The two fictitious processing times P_i^A and P_i^B for each job are calculated as $[(P_1^A, P_1^B), (P_2^A, P_2^B), (P_3^A, P_3^B), (P_4^A, P_4^B)] = [(20, 23), (36, 32), (24, 25), (25, 32)]$ (For example, $P_1^A = p_1^1 + p_1^2 + p_1^3 = 5 + 3 + 12 = 20$ and $P_1^B = p_1^3 + p_1^4 + p_1^5 = 12 + 4 + 7 = 23$).

Applying Johnson's algorithm to these P_i^A's and P_i^B's, the job sequence $J_1 - J_3 - J_4 - J_2$ is easily obtained. The makespan of this schedule is 76. Considering that the makespan of the optimal one obtained by the branch-and-bound algorithm is 74, it is said that the schedule determined by Petrov's method would give a fairly good result with much less computational time.

8.1.4 Job-Shop Scheduling Problem

Job-shop scheduling problems are much more complicated than flow-shop scheduling problems, since the flow of the jobs to be processed on machines is not unidirectional. Job-shop scheduling problems have not yet been solved theoretically except some very simple ones. One of the simple problems that has been solved is a two-job job-shop scheduling problem for which a graphical procedure has been proposed.

For general job-shop scheduling problems, general purpose methodologies such as the branch-and-bound method and integer programming are applicable to solve. However, computational efforts to determine optimal schedules are not small even for the medium sized problems; therefore, such methods are not practical for solving the problems that occur in actual situations, which often include a large number of jobs and machines.

This subsection describes one specialized type of integer programming structure that is useful in solving job-shop scheduling problems [11]. Let us consider the minimum makespan problem of scheduling n jobs on m machines in a job shop. Let x_i^k denote the completion time of job i (J_i) on machine k (M_k) when the particular operation of J_i requires machine M_k. Supposing that two successive operations $j - 1$ and j of J_i require machines M_h and M_k, respectively, it is necessary to have:

$$x_i^k - p_{ij}^k \geq x_i^h \, (i = 1, 2, \ldots, n, j = 1, 2, \ldots, m) \qquad (8.17)$$

where p_{ij}^k is the processing time of the jth operation for J_i on M_k. For the first operation ($j = 1$), the constraint is simply:

$$x_i^k - p_{i1}^k \geq 0 \, (i = 1, 2, \ldots, n) \qquad (8.18)$$

In many job-shop scheduling problems, there are precedence constraints among jobs. When J_i precedes J_p on M_k (which means the operation j of J_i is completed before the operation q of J_p begins), the following constraints must be satisfied:

$$x_p^k - x_i^k + H(1 - y_{ip}^k) \geq p_{pq}^k \qquad (8.19)$$

$$x_i^k - x_p^k + Hy_{ip}^k \geq p_{ij}^k \qquad (8.20)$$

where y_{ip}^k is an indicator variable defined as:

$$y_{ip}^k = \begin{cases} 1, \text{ if } J_i \text{ precedes } J_p \text{ on } M_k \\ 0, \text{ otherwise} \end{cases} \qquad (8.21)$$

and H represents a very large positive number.

The scheduling criterion is the minimization of the makespan. The makespan must be at least as large as the completion time of the last operation of any job, so that

$$y \geq x_i^{k_i} \, (i = 1, 2, \ldots, n) \qquad (8.22)$$

where k_i denotes the machine at which the last operation of J_i is scheduled. For the makespan problem, the entire formulation is:
Minimize

$$y \qquad (8.23)$$

subject to

$$x_i^k - p_{ij}^k \geq x_i^h \, (i = 1, 2, \ldots, n, j = 1, 2, \ldots, m)$$

$$x_p^k - x_i^k + H(1 - y_{ip}^k) \geq p_{pq}^k \left(\begin{array}{l} i, p = 1, 2, \ldots, n \\ j = 1, 2, \ldots m \end{array} \right)$$

$$x_i^k - x_p^k + Hy_{ip}^k \geq p_{ij}^k \left(\begin{array}{l} i, p = 1, 2, \ldots, n \\ j = 1, 2, \ldots m \end{array} \right)$$

$$y \geq x_i^{k_i} \ (i = 1, 2, \ldots, n)$$

In the above formulation, there are mn constraints of inequalities (8.17) or (8.18), $mn(n - 1)$ of inequalities (8.19) or (8.20), and n of inequalities (8.22), or a total of $mn^2 + n$ constraints. There are mn x_i^k variables and $mn(n - 1)/2$ y_{ip}^k variables. The total number of variables is therefore $mn(n + 1)/2$.

In the case that the minimization of the mean flow time is employed as a scheduling criterion, the following objective function is given, instead of equation 8.23.

Minimize

$$y = \sum_{i=1}^{n} x_i^{k_i} \tag{8.24}$$

In this case, there are mn^2 constraints and $mn(n + 1)/2$ variables, the same number of variables as the case of the minimum makespan problem.

For either of the two cases, not a less computational effort is required to solve even medium-sized scheduling problems.

8.2 Multi-Stage Group Production Scheduling

In chapter 7, a group scheduling problem of a single machine was defined and analyzed under the criteria of minimizing the mean flow time and the weighted mean flow time. This section treats a multi-stage group production scheduling problem. Even for group production scheduling problems, various kinds of scheduling criteria will be considered. However, as in the case of the conventional flow-shop scheduling problems, multi-stage group production scheduling problems are intractable for most of the scheduling criteria. Therefore, the scheduling criterion primarily employed in this chapter is that of minimizing the makespan (total elapsed time).

Consider the problem of scheduling N groups, each of which consists of n_i jobs, in a flow shop that consists of K machines. Let $p_{i\xi}^k$ ($i = 1, 2, \ldots, N$, $\xi = 1, 2, \ldots, n_i$, $k = 1, 2, \ldots, K$) denote job processing time including job setup time on stage (machine) M_k ($k = 1, 2, \ldots, K$) of job $J_{i\xi}$ ($i = 1, 2, \ldots, N$, $\xi = 1, 2, \ldots, n_i$) of group G_i ($i = 1, 2, \ldots, N$) and S_i^k ($i = 1$,

$2, \ldots, N$, $k = 1, 2, \ldots, K$) denote the group setup time on stage M_k of group G_i.

The problem to be solved is to determine an optimal group schedule (optimal group sequence and optimal job sequences in groups) that minimizes the makespan. In the later section, the problem is solved by three kinds of approaches: theoretical [12, 13], branch-and-bound [14], and heuristic [15].

8.3 Theoretical Approach to Group Scheduling

8.3.1 Two-Machine Flow-Shop Group Scheduling

In the case of conventional scheduling problems in which there is only one group consisting of n jobs to be processed, Johnson's problem is fundamentally standard. Johnson's theorem and algorithm for the two-machine flow-shop scheduling problem minimizing the makespan can be extended to group scheduling.

In the two-stage flow-shop group scheduling for the minimum makespan, the following theorem can be proven in the same manner as in the lemma by Johnson.

Theorem 8.7. For the two-stage flow-shop group scheduling problem of minimizing the makespan, it is sufficient to consider only group schedules in which the same orders of groups and jobs occur on both machines.

First, develop the recursive relation of the completion time on machine M_k of job $J_{(i)(\xi)}$, which indicates the ξth job in the ith group in a group schedule. The completion time of $J_{(i)(\xi)}$ on M_k is given by

$$\left. \begin{array}{l} C^k_{(i)(\xi)} = \max(C^{k-1}_{(i)(\xi)}, C^k_{(i)(\xi-1)}) + p^k_{(i)(\xi)}, \text{ if } \xi \neq 1 \\[2mm] C^k_{(i)(1)} = \max(C^{k-1}_{(i)(1)}, C^k_{(i-1)(n_{i-1})} + S^k_{(i)}) + p^k_{(i)(1)}, \text{ if } \xi = 1 \end{array} \right\} \quad (8.25)$$

where

$$C^0_{(i)(\xi)} = C^k_{(0)(n_0)} = 0.$$

By repeatedly using these recursive relations, the makespan for the two-stage flow-shop problem—that is, the completion time on M_2 of $J_{(N)(n_N)}$—is expressed as:

$$F_{\max} = C^2_{(N)(n_N)} = \max_{0 \leq u \leq N} \max_{1 \leq v \leq n_u} \left\{ \sum_{i=1}^{u-1} \left(S^1_{(i)} + \sum_{\xi=1}^{n(i)} p^1_{(i)(\xi)} \right) + S^1_{(u)} \right.$$

$$+ \sum_{\xi=1}^{v} p^1_{(u)(\xi)} + \sum_{\xi=v}^{n(u)} p^2_{(u)(\xi)} + \sum_{i=u+1}^{N} \left(S^2_{(i)} + \sum_{\xi=1}^{n(i)} p^2_{(i)(\xi)} \right) \Bigg\}$$

$$= \max_{0 \le u \le N} \left\{ \sum_{i=1}^{u-1} (S^1_{(i)} + P^1_{(i)}) + S^1_{(u)} + \max_{1 \le v \le n_u} \left(\sum_{\xi=1}^{v} p^1_{(u)(\xi)} \right. \right.$$

$$\left. + \sum_{\xi=v}^{n(u)} p^2_{(u)(\xi)} \right) + \sum_{i=u+1}^{N} (S^2_{(i)} + P^2_{(i)}) \Bigg\} \tag{8.26}$$

where $P^k_{(i)} = \sum_{\xi=1}^{n(i)} p^k_{(i)(\xi)}$, $p^k_{(0)(\xi)} = 0$ $(k = 1, 2)$, $S^1_{(0)} = 0$, and $n_{(0)} \ge 1$.

The problem is to determine a group schedule so as to minimize the above equation. The following theorem holds for this problem.

Theorem 8.8. For the two-stage flow-shop group scheduling problem for the minimum makespan, an optimal group schedule is obtained by the following rules: the job sequence, by rule 1, and the group sequence, by rule 2.

Rule 1. Job $J_{i\xi}$ precedes job $J_{i\eta}$ if

$$\min(p^1_{i\xi}, p^2_{i\eta}) < \min(p^1_{i\eta}, p^2_{i\xi}) \tag{8.27}$$

Rule 2. Group G_i precedes group G_j if

$$\min \left\{ S^1_i - S^2_i + \max_{1 \le v \le n_i} \left(\sum_{\xi=1}^{v} p^1_{i\xi} - \sum_{\xi=1}^{v-1} p^2_{i\xi} \right), \max_{1 \le v \le n_j} \left(\sum_{\xi=v}^{n_j} p^2_{j\xi} \right. \right.$$

$$\left. - \sum_{\xi=v+1}^{n_j} p^1_{j\xi} \right) \Bigg\} < \min \left\{ S^1_j - S^2_j + \max_{1 \le v \le n_j} \left(\sum_{\xi=1}^{v} p^1_{j\xi} \right. \right.$$

$$\left. - \sum_{\xi=1}^{v-1} p^2_{j\xi} \right), \max_{1 \le v \le n_i} \left(\sum_{\xi=v}^{n_i} p^2_{i\xi} - \sum_{\xi=v+1}^{n_i} p^1_{i\xi} \right) \Bigg\} \tag{8.28}$$

If there is equality in inequality (8.27) or (8.28), either ordering is optimal for group and job sequences, respectively.

This theorem is an extension of Johnson's and also an extension of the string problem's to group scheduling. With the use of this theorem, a simple algorithm for determining an optimal group schedule is developed as follows:

Optimizing algorithm for the two-stage flow-shop group scheduling.

Step 1. Determine an optimal job sequence in each group by using Johnson's working rule.

Step 2. Determine an optimal group sequence in the following way:

1. Calculate the following values for each group under the job sequences determined by step 1.

$$X_i = S_i^1 - S_i^2 + \max_{1 \le v \le n_i} \left(\sum_{\xi=1}^{v} p_{i\xi}^1 - \sum_{\xi=1}^{v-1} p_{i\xi}^2 \right)$$

$$Y_i = \max_{1 \le v \le n_i} \left(\sum_{\xi=v}^{n_i} p_{i\xi}^2 - \sum_{\xi=v+1}^{n_i} p_{i\xi}^1 \right)$$

2. Find the minimum value among the X_i's and the Y_i's. (In the case of a tie, select arbitrarily).
3. If it is X_a, place G_a first, and if it is Y_a, place G_a last.
4. Remove the assigned group from consideration and go back to 2.

Example 8.6. By using the optimizing algorithm developed, determine an optimal group schedule for a seven-job, three-group, two-stage problem given by table 8.6.

Step 1. By applying Johnson's working rule to job processing times of each group, optimal job sequences are determined as $J_{11} - J_{12}$, $J_{22} - J_{21} - J_{23}$, and $J_{32} - J_{31}$, respectively.

Step 2. The values of X_i and Y_i for each group are calculated as: $[(X_1, Y_1), (X_2, Y_2), (X_3, Y_3)] = [(7, 8), (8, 6), (4, 6)]$. For example,

Table 8.6. Production data for a seven-job, three-group, two-stage group scheduling problem in hours

Group	G_1			G_2				G_3		
Job		J_{11}	J_{12}		J_{21}	J_{22}	J_{23}		J_{31}	J_{32}
Setup time/ processing time	S_1^k	p_{11}^k	p_{12}^k	S_2^k	p_{21}^k	p_{22}^k	p_{23}^k	S_3^k	p_{31}^k	p_{32}^k
Stage M_1	3	5	8	3	8	5	10	1	9	3
Stage M_2	1	9	7	2	7	9	6	2	6	7

$X_1 = 3 - 1 + \max(5, \ 5 + 8 - 9) = 7$ and $Y_1 = \max(9 + 7 - 8, \ 7) = 8$. From these values, an optimal group sequence is easily determined as $G_3 - G_1 - G_2$.

Consequently, the optimal group schedule is $G_3(J_{32} - J_{31}) - G_1(J_{11} - J_{12}) - G_2(J_{22} - J_{21} - J_{23})$ with the makespan of 61 hours.

8.3.2 Optimal Group Scheduling on Multiple Production Stages

The recent advances in scheduling techniques have shown that it is rather difficult to develop simple optimizing algorithms for solving the large-scale (or multi-stage) general flow-shop scheduling problem with even a simple criterion of minimizing the makespan, much less the problems with more complex measures, such as minimizing the mean flow time. As a result of this awareness, a direction of recent theoretical research in multi-stage scheduling problems has been turned to the special structure scheduling problems that can be easily solved. Special structure problems in the conventional scheduling have been treated in the previous section. In this subsection, they are generalized to group scheduling. A theoretical determination of the optimal group schedule under the criterion of the minimum makespan can be made to the special structure flow-shop scheduling problems where there exist some well-defined relationships among the group setup times and the job processing times.

For the K-stage flow-shop group scheduling problem ($K \geq 3$), the schedules having the same order of groups and jobs on the first two machines include an optimal schedule under the criterion of minimizing the makespan, while the optimal schedule does not always have the same order on the last two machines. The latter property does not occur because of the grouping of jobs into several groups but because of the feature of the group setup time.

In the K-stage flow-shop group scheduling problem which will be treated hereafter, it is assumed that the processing order of groups and jobs is the same on each machine. (No passing of groups and jobs is allowed.)

In general, the task of determining a schedule so as to minimize the makespan is formidable. However, if each of the following well-defined relationships holds among the group setup times and the job processing times at each of the stages, the problem can be reduced to a two-stage one and solved theoretically.

Case 1: For a fixed $h \leq (K - 1)$, the group setup times and the job processing times satisfy the following conditions:

(i) $\min\limits_{1\le i\le N} (S_i^k - S_i^{k+1} + \min\limits_{1\le \xi\le n_i} p_{i\xi}^k) \ge \max\limits_{1\le j\le N} \max\limits_{1\le \eta\le n_j} p_{j\eta}^{k+1}$

$\left.\begin{array}{c} \\ \\ \\ \\ \end{array}\right\}$ $\begin{array}{c} \forall k \le h - 1 \\ \le K - 2 \end{array}$

      $\min\limits_{1\le \xi\le n_i} p_{i\xi}^k \ge \max\limits_{1\le \eta\le n_i} p_{i\eta}^{k+1} \quad (i = 1, 2, \ldots, N)$

(ii) $\max\limits_{1\le i\le N} (S_i^k - S_i^{k+1} + \max\limits_{1\le \xi\le n_i} p_{i\xi}^k) \le \min\limits_{1\le j\le N} \min\limits_{1\le \eta\le n_j} p_{j\eta}^{k+1}$

$\left.\begin{array}{c} \\ \\ \\ \\ \end{array}\right\}$ $\begin{array}{c} h + 1 \le \forall k \\ \le K - 1 \end{array}$

      $\max\limits_{1\le \xi\le n_i} p_{i\xi}^k \le \min\limits_{1\le \eta\le n_i} p_{i\eta}^{k+1} \quad (i = 1, 2, \ldots, N)$

$$(8.29)$$

Case 2: The group setup times and the job processing times satisfy the following conditions:

$\max\limits_{1\le i\le N} (S_i^k - S_i^{k+1} + \max\limits_{1\le \xi\le n_i} p_{i\xi}^k) \le \min\limits_{1\le j\le N} \min\limits_{1\le \eta\le n_j} p_{j\eta}^{k+1}$

$\left.\begin{array}{c} \\ \\ \\ \\ \end{array}\right\}$ $\forall k \le K - 2$

$\max\limits_{1\le \xi\le n_i} p_{i\xi}^k \le \min\limits_{1\le \eta\le n_i} p_{i\eta}^{k+1} \quad (i = 1, 2, \ldots, N)$

$$(8.30)$$

Case 3: The group setup times and the job processing times satisfy the following conditions:

$\min\limits_{1\le i\le N} (S_i^k - S_i^{k+1} + \min\limits_{1\le \xi\le n_i} p_{i\xi}^k) \ge \max\limits_{1\le j\le N} \max\limits_{1\le \eta\le n_j} p_{j\eta}^{k+1}$

$\left.\begin{array}{c} \\ \\ \\ \\ \end{array}\right\}$ $\begin{array}{c} 2 \le \forall k \\ \le K - 1 \end{array}$

$\min\limits_{1\le \xi\le n_i} p_{i\xi}^k \ge \max\limits_{1\le \eta\le n_i} p_{i\eta}^{k+1} \quad (i = 1, 2, \ldots, N)$

$$(8.31)$$

Note that none of the above conditions is required when $K = 2$. The following theorem holds for case 1.

Theorem 8.9. If the group setup times and the job processing times satisfy condition 8.29, then an optimal group schedule is obtained by determining the job sequence for each group using rule 1 and the group sequence using rule 2.

Rule 1:   Job $J_{i\xi}$ precedes job $J_{i\eta}$ if

$$\min \left(\sum_{k=1}^{K-1} p_{i\xi}^k, \sum_{k=2}^{K} p_{i\eta}^k \right) < \min \left(\sum_{k=1}^{K-1} p_{i\eta}^k, \sum_{k=2}^{K} p_{i\xi}^k \right) \qquad (8.32)$$

Rule 2:   Group G_i precedes group G_j if

$$\min \left\{ \sum_{k=1}^{K-1} S_i^k - \sum_{k=2}^{K} S_i^k + \max_{1 \le v \le n_i} \left(\sum_{\xi=1}^{v} \sum_{k=1}^{K-1} p_{i\xi}^k - \sum_{\xi=1}^{v-1} \sum_{k=2}^{K} p_{i\xi}^k \right), \right.$$

$$\left. \max_{1 \le v \le n_j} \left(\sum_{\xi=v}^{n_j} \sum_{k=2}^{K} p_{j\xi}^k - \sum_{\xi=v+1}^{n_j} \sum_{k=1}^{K-1} p_{j\xi}^k \right) \right\}$$

$$< \min \left\{ \sum_{k=1}^{K-1} S_j^k - \sum_{k=2}^{K} S_j^k + \max_{1 \le v \le n_j} \left(\sum_{\xi=1}^{v} \sum_{k=1}^{K-1} p_{j\xi}^k - \sum_{\xi=1}^{v-1} \sum_{k=2}^{K} p_{j\xi}^k \right), \right.$$

$$\left. \max_{1 \le v \le n_i} \left(\sum_{\xi=v}^{n_i} \sum_{k=2}^{K} p_{i\xi}^k - \sum_{\xi=v+1}^{n_i} \sum_{k=1}^{K-1} p_{i\xi}^k \right) \right\} \qquad (8.33)$$

If there is equality in inequality 8.32 or 8.33, either ordering is optimal for group and job sequences, respectively.

With the help of this theorem, an optimal group schedule can be determined easily by the following algorithm similar to the one for the two-stage problem, since rules 1 and 2 have the same forms as the rules of theorem 8.8.

Optimizing algorithm for case 1

Step 1. (Determining the optimal job sequences)
1. Calculate the fictitious processing times, the values of $\Sigma_{k=1}^{K-1} p_{i\xi}^k (=x_{i\xi})$ and $\Sigma_{k=2}^{K} p_{i\xi}^k (=y_{i\xi})$ for each job.
2. Determine an optimal job sequence for each group by applying Johnson's working rule to these values.
Step 2. (Determining the optimal group sequence)
1. Calculate the following values for each group under the job sequences determined by step 1.

$$X_i = \sum_{k=1}^{K-1} S_i^k - \sum_{k=2}^{K} S_i^k + \max_{1 \le v \le n_i} \left(\sum_{\xi=1}^{v} \sum_{k=1}^{K-1} p_{i\xi}^k - \sum_{\xi=1}^{v-1} \sum_{k=2}^{K} p_{i\xi}^k \right)$$

$$Y_i = \max_{1 \le v \le n_i} \left(\sum_{\xi=v}^{n_i} \sum_{k=2}^{K} p_{i\xi}^k - \sum_{\xi=v+1}^{n_i} \sum_{k=1}^{K-1} p_{i\xi}^k \right)$$

2. Find the minimum value among the X_i's and the Y_i's. (In case of a tie, select arbitrarily.)
3. If it is X_a, place G_a first, and if it is Y_a, place G_a last.
4. Remove the assigned group from consideration and go back to 2.

For cases 2 and 3, the optimizing algorithms for determining an optimal group schedule are proposed as follows:

Optimizing algorithm for case 2.

Step 1. Determine an optimal group schedule, S, for the two-stage problem (stages M_{K-1} and M_K). Let $J_{a\alpha}$ be the first job of schedule S.
Step 2. Let $\Pi = (J_{i_1\xi_1}, J_{i_2\xi_2}, \ldots, J_{i_l\xi_l})$ be a set of jobs such that

$$\max_{0 \le u_1 \le u_2 \le \ldots \le u_{K-2}=1} \sum_{k=1}^{K-2} \sum_{i_j=1}^{u_k} (S_{i_j}^k - S_{i_j}^{k+1} + p_{i_j\xi_j}^k)$$

$$< \max_{0 \le u_1 \le u_2 \le \ldots \le u_{K-2}=1} \sum_{k=1}^{K-2} \sum_{i=1}^{u_k} (S_a^k - S_a^{k+1} + p_{a\alpha}^k)$$

Generate l new group schedules by assigning, first, each group containing the jobs $J_{i_j\xi_j}$ $(\in \Pi)$ to the first position, and then placing each job $J_{i_j\xi_j}$ first in the job sequence of G_{i_j} and maintaining the schedule S order for the remaining groups and jobs.
Step 3. Among the $(l+1)$ schedules obtained above, find the group schedule minimizing the total elapsed time. This schedule is optimal.

Optimizing algorithm for case 3.

Step 1. Determine an optimal group schedule S, for the two-stage problem (stages M_1 and M_2). Let $J_{z\beta}$ be the last job of schedule S.
Step 2. Let $\Pi = (J_{i_1\xi_1}, J_{i_2\xi_2}, \ldots, J_{i_l\xi_l})$ be a set of jobs such that

$$\sum_{k=3}^{K} p_{i_j\xi_j}^k < \sum_{k=3}^{K} p_{z\beta}^k$$

Generate l new group schedules by assigning, first, each group G_{ij} containing the jobs $J_{ij\xi_j}$ ($\in\Pi$) to the last position, and then placing each job $J_{ij\xi_j}$ last in the job sequence of G_{ij} and maintaining the schedule S order for the remaining groups and jobs.

Step 3. Among the $(l+1)$ schedules obtained above, find the group schedule minimizing the total elapsed time. This schedule is optimal.

To illustrate the optimizing algorithms presented, consider two special structure flow-shop group scheduling problems.

Example 8.7. The production data for a 10-job, 4-group, 4-stage problem are given in table 8.7. This is an example of case 1, since the group setup times and the job processing times satisfy condition 8.29 for $h = 3$ as follows:

$$\min_{1\le i\le 4} \left(S_i^1 - S_i^2 + \min_{1\le\xi\le n_i} p_{i\xi}^1\right)(= 15) \ge \max_{1\le j\le 4}\ \max_{1\le\eta\le n_j} p_{j\eta}^2(= 15)$$

$$\min_{1\le\xi\le 2} p_{1\xi}^1(= 16) \ge \max_{1\le\eta\le 2} p_{1\eta}^2(= 15)$$

$$\min_{1\le\xi\le 3} p_{2\xi}^1(= 15) \ge \max_{1\le\eta\le 3} p_{2\eta}^2(= 14)$$

$$\min_{1\le\xi\le 2} p_{3\xi}^1(= 15) \ge \max_{1\le\eta\le 2} p_{3\eta}^2(= 15)$$

$$\min_{1\le\xi\le 3} p_{4\xi}^1(= 16) \ge \max_{1\le\eta\le 3} p_{4\eta}^2(= 15)$$

$$\min_{1\le i\le 4} \left(S_i^2 - S_i^3 + \min_{1\le\xi\le n_i} p_{i\xi}^2\right)(= 11) \ge \max_{1\le j\le N}\ \max_{1\le\eta\le n_j} p_{j\eta}^3(= 10)$$

Table 8.7. Production data for Example 8.7 in hours

Group	G_1		G_2			G_3		G_4		
Job	J_{11}	J_{12}	J_{21}	J_{22}	J_{23}	J_{31}	J_{32}	J_{41}	J_{42}	J_{43}
Setup time / processing time	S_1^k p_{11}^k p_{12}^k		S_2^k p_{21}^k p_{22}^k p_{23}^k			S_3^k p_{31}^k p_{32}^k		S_4^k p_{41}^k p_{42}^k p_{43}^k		
Stage M_1	5	16	18	3	18	19	15	4	15	19	4	17	16	20
Stage M_2	4	15	13	3	12	14	11	3	10	15	5	10	13	15
Stage M_3	3	6	10	4	10	8	7	2	6	8	3	5	10	9
Stage M_4	4	13	20	4	15	6	17	5	18	20	4	12	9	17

$$\min_{1\le\xi\le2} p^2_{1\xi}(=13) \ge \max_{1\le\eta\le2} p^3_{1\eta}(=10)$$

$$\min_{1\le\xi\le3} p^2_{2\xi}(=11) \ge \max_{1\le\eta\le3} p^3_{2\eta}(=10)$$

$$\min_{1\le\xi\le2} p^2_{3\xi}(=10) \ge \max_{1\le\eta\le2} p^3_{3\eta}(=8)$$

$$\min_{1\le\xi\le3} p^2_{4\xi}(=10) \ge \max_{1\le\eta\le3} p^3_{4\eta}(=10)$$

Thus the optimal group schedule is determined by using the optimizing algorithm for case 1.

Step 1. The values of $x_{i\xi}$ and $y_{i\xi}$ for each job are computed as in table 8.8. By applying Johnson's working rule to this table, the optimal job sequences for four groups are decided as $J_{12} - J_{11}$, $J_{23} - J_{21} - J_{22}$, $J_{31} - J_{32}$, and $J_{43} - J_{42} - J_{41}$, respectively.

Step 2. The values of X_i and Y_i for each group are calculated as: $[(X_1, Y_1), (X_2, Y_2), (X_3, Y_3), (X_4, Y_4)] = [(42, 40), (41, 28), (38, 39), (44, 29)]$ (for example, $X_1 = 5 - 4 + \max(41, 31 + 37 - 43) = 42$ and $X_2 = \max(43 + 34 - 37, 34) = 40$). Hence, from this list, the optimal group sequence is $G_3 - G_1 - G_4 - G_2$.

Consequently, the optimal group schedule is determined as $G_3(J_{31} - J_{32}) - G_1(J_{12} - J_{11}) - G_4(J_{43} - J_{42} - J_{41}) - G_2(J_{23} - J_{21} - J_{22})$ with the makespan of 217 hours. The Gantt chart of this schedule is given by figure 8.9.

Example 8.8.   The production data for a 10-job, 4-group, 4-stage problem are given in table 8.9. The group setup times and the job processing times satisfy condition 8.30 of case 2 as follows:

$$\max_{1\le i\le4} \left(S^1_i - S^2_i + \max_{1\le\xi\le n_i} p^1_{i\xi}\right)(=10) \le \min_{1\le j\le4} \min_{1\le\eta\le n_j} p^2_{j\eta}(=10)$$

$$\max_{1\le\xi\le2} p^1_{1\xi}(=10) \le \min_{1\le\eta\le2} p^2_{1\eta}(=12)$$

Table 8.8.   List of $x_{i\xi}$ and $y_{i\xi}$
(units: hours)

Group	G_1		G_2			G_3		G_4		
Job	J_{11}	J_{12}	J_{21}	J_{22}	J_{23}	J_{31}	J_{32}	J_{41}	J_{42}	J_{43}
$x_{i\xi}$	37	41	40	41	33	31	42	32	39	43
$y_{i\xi}$	34	43	37	28	35	34	43	27	32	41

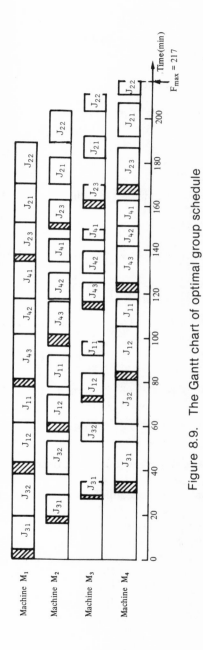

Figure 8.9. The Gantt chart of optimal group schedule

Table 8.9. Production data for Example 8.8 in hours

Group	G_1		G_2			G_3		G_4		
Job	J_{11} J_{12}		J_{21} J_{22} J_{23}			J_{31} J_{32}		J_{41} J_{42}		J
Setup time/										
Processing time	S_1^k p_{11}^k p_{12}^k		S_2^k p_{21}^k p_{22}^k p_{23}^k			S_3^k p_{31}^k p_{32}^k		S_4^k p_{41}^k p_{42}^k		p
Stage M_1	2	6	10	3	9	5	8	1	7	8	2	9	6
Stage M_2	3	14	12	2	10	11	15	2	13	11	2	13	5	1
Stage M_3	4	18	16	3	17	19	18	2	16	15	4	18	20	1
Stage M_4	2	9	19	4	22	12	25	3	20	23	3	9	13	1

$$\max_{1\le \xi \le 3} p_{2\xi}^1 \ (=9) \le \min_{1\le \eta \le 3} p_{2\eta}^2 (=10)$$

$$\max_{1\le \xi \le 2} p_{3\xi}^1 \ (=8) \le \min_{1\le \eta \le 2} p_{3\eta}^2 (=11)$$

$$\max_{1\le \xi \le 3} p_{4\xi}^1 \ (=9) \le \min_{1\le \eta \le 3} p_{4\eta}^2 (=10)$$

$$\max_{1\le i \le 4} \left(S_i^2 - S_i^3 + \max_{1\le \xi \le n_i} p_{i\xi}^2 \right)(=14) \le \min_{1\le j \le 4} \min_{1\le \eta \le n_j} p_{j\eta}^3 (=15)$$

$$\max_{1\le \xi \le 2} p_{1\xi}^2 (=14) \le \min_{1\le \eta \le 2} p_{1\eta}^3 (=16)$$

$$\max_{1\le \xi \le 3} p_{2\xi}^2 (=15) \le \min_{1\le \eta \le 3} p_{2\eta}^3 (=17)$$

$$\max_{1\le \xi \le 2} p_{3\xi}^2 (=13) \le \min_{1\le \eta \le 2} p_{3\eta}^3 (=15)$$

$$\max_{1\le \xi \le 3} p_{4\xi}^2 (=15) \le \min_{1\le \eta \le 3} p_{4\eta}^3 (=18)$$

Hence, the optimal group schedule is obtained by using the optimizing algorithm for case 2.

Step 1. The optimal group schedule for the two-stage problem (stages M_3 and M_4) is determined as $G_3(J_{32} - J_{31}) - G_2(J_{21} - J_{23} - J_{22}) - G_1(J_{12} - J_{11}) - G_4(J_{42} - J_{43} - J_{41})$. Thus $J_{a\alpha} = J_{32}$.

Step 2. The values of $\max_{0\le u_1 \le u_2 = 1} \Sigma_{k=1}^2 \Sigma_{i=1}^{u_k} (S_i^k - S_i^{k+1} + p_{i\xi}^k)(=z_{i\xi})$ for each job are computed as: $[(z_{11}, z_{12}), (z_{21}, z_{22}, z_{23}), (z_{31}, z_{32}), (z_{41}, z_{42}, z_{43})] = [(18, 20), (19, 16, 23), (19, 18), (20, 19, 15)]$ (for example, $z_{11} = \max(S_1^2 - S_1^3 + p_{11}^2, \ S_1^1 - S_1^2 + p_{11}^1 + S_1^2 - S_1^3 + p_{11}^2) = 18$). $\Pi = \{J_{22}, J_{43}\}$, since $z_{32} = 18$. Therefore, it is necessary to evaluate the following three schedules to determine the optimal group schedule.

Schedule S: $\quad G_3(J_{32} - J_{31}) - G_2(J_{21} - J_{23} - J_{22}) - G_1(J_{12} - J_{11})$

$\qquad\qquad - G_4(J_{42} - J_{43} - J_{41})$

Schedule S_{22}: $\quad G_2(J_{22} - J_{21} - J_{23}) - G_3(J_{32} - J_{31}) - G_1(J_{12} - J_{11})$

$\qquad\qquad - G_4(J_{42} - J_{43} - J_{41})$

Schedule S_{43}: $\quad G_4(J_{43} - J_{42} - J_{41}) - G_3(J_{32} - J_{31}) - G_2(J_{21} - J_{23} - J_{22})$

$\qquad\qquad - G_1(J_{12} - J_{11})$

Step 3. Since the makespans for the above three schedules are 216, 212, and 229 hours, respectively, the optimal group schedule is the schedule S_{22}.

8.4 Branch-and-Bound Approach to Group Scheduling

As stated in the previous section, a successful analysis of a multi-stage scheduling problem is limited to the case of the two-stage flow-shop problem with the objective of minimizing the makespan. For flow-shop scheduling problems of three machines or more, a universal theoretical analysis cannot be made even under the simple criterion of the minimum makespan. In order to generally solve the problems, it is necessary to resort to general purpose methodologies, such as a dynamic programming approach, a branch-and-bound method, et cetera, or a heuristic procedure.

Among these, as shown in chapter 7, the branch-and-bound method has been employed with some success for the conventional flow-shop scheduling problems. With the help of the branch-and-bound method, the flow-shop group scheduling problems of minimizing the makespan are solved in this section. In these problems, the ordering of groups and jobs is also assumed to be the same on each machine. For the minimum makespan flow-shop problem, three kinds of lower bounds will be shown by extending the typical ones in the conventional scheduling to the group scheduling. Then an optimizing algorithm that incorporates these bounds is presented.

First, by using the idle times of jobs on the last stage, we develop the expression of the makespan to be minimized.

The completion time on M_k of $J_{(i)(\xi)}$ indicating the ξth job in the ith group in a group schedule is shown as

$$C_{(i)(\xi)}^k = \sum_{j=1}^{i-1} \left(\sum_{\eta=1}^{n_{(j)}} g_{(j)(\eta)}^k + S_{(j)}^k + P_{(j)}^k \right) + S_{(i)}^k$$

$$+ \sum_{\eta=1}^{\xi} (g^k_{(i)(\eta)} + p^k_{(i)(\eta)}) \tag{8.34}$$

where $P^k_{(i)} = \sum_{\xi=1}^{n(i)} p^k_{(i)(\xi)}$ and $g^k_{(i)(\xi)}$ is the idle time of M_k before processing ξth job after completion of $(\xi - 1)$th job of $G_{(i)}$, and is given as follows:

$$g^k_{(i)(\xi)} = \begin{cases} C^{k-1}_{(i)(\xi)} - C^k_{(i)(\xi-1)}, & \text{if } C^{k-1}_{(i)(\xi)} > C^k_{(i)(\xi-1)} \\ 0, & \text{otherwise} \end{cases}$$

for $\xi \neq 1$ and

$$g^k_{(i)(1)} = \begin{cases} C^{k-1}_{(i)(1)} - C^k_{(i-1)(n_{i-1})} - S^k_{(i)}, & \text{if } C^{k-1}_{(i)(1)} > C^k_{(i-1)(n_{i-1})} + S^k_{(i)} \\ 0, & \text{otherwise} \end{cases}$$

for $\xi = 1$. Hence, the makespan is given by:

$$F_{\max} = C^K_{(N)(n_N)}$$

$$= \sum_{i=1}^{N} \left(\sum_{\xi=1}^{n(i)} g^K_{(i)(\xi)} + S^K_{(i)} + P^K_{(i)} \right) \tag{8.35}$$

Now the branch-and-bound method is applied to solve a flow-shop group scheduling problem. Since, in group scheduling, both optimal group and job sequences must be determined simultaneously, a new type of branch-and-bound procedure is required.

The basic branching procedure for the group scheduling is as follows: In group scheduling, branching of groups and branching of jobs are both required, since optimal decisions are made as to the sequences of groups and of jobs in each group. Eventually, there occur two kinds of nodes—: "group node" and "job node." Basically, the branching of groups is made first by taking each of the unsequenced groups in turn and placing it next in the permutation of groups already determined. Then, in the same way, jobs are branched from each of the group nodes created. The procedure for branching of jobs in the current group is repeated until the positions of all jobs in the group are determined. After that, new group nodes are created by branching unallocated groups at each of the job nodes.

Let N_r be a group node at which the sequence of r groups is specified: $N_r = [G_{(1)}, G_{(2)}, \ldots, G_{(r)}]$ and N_{rs} be a job node at which s jobs in group $G_{(r)}$ are allocated: $N_{rs} = [J_{(r)(1)}, J_{(r)(2)}, \ldots, J_{(r)(s)}]$. Then N_r and N_{rs} are called r-level group node and s-level job node, respectively.

After branching of groups at N_r, $(n - r)$ group nodes are created by placing each of the unsequenced groups, $G_{(r+1)}$, next in the permutation already sequenced; $N_{r+1} = [G_{(1)}, G_{(2)}, \ldots, G_{(r)}, G_{(r+1)}]$. Branching of the job node at N_{rs} is made by placing each of the jobs not yet allocated in group $G_{(r)}$, $J_{(r)(s+1)}$, next in the permutation already sequenced; thus $(n_{(r)} - s)$ new job nodes, $N_{rs+1} = [J_{(r)(1)}, J_{(r)(2)}, \ldots, J_{(r)(s)}, J_{(r)(s+1)}]$, are created. the process of branching of groups and jobs is shown in figure 8.10.

The bounding procedure is a process of calculating the lower bound on the solution of the subproblem represented by each job node. The formula for the lower bound depends on the scheduling criterion employed.

A variety of lower bounds on the makespan have been developed for the conventional flow-shop scheduling problem as described in the previous chapter. Representative of these bounds are the machine-based, the job-based, and the composite bounds. For determining the optimal group schedule, the lower bounds can be developed by extending the above three bounds to the group scheduling, as follows:

1. Machine-based bound: The machine-based bound at N_{rs} is estimated by:

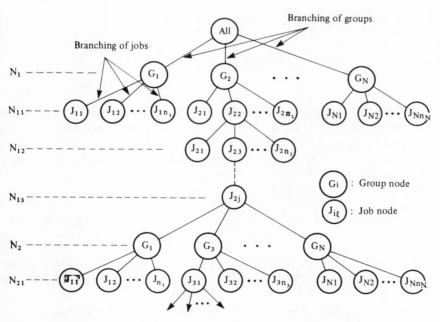

Figure 8.10. The branching process for group scheduling problems

$$L_1(N_{rs}) = \max_{1 \leq k \leq K} \left\{ C^k_{(r)(s)} + \sum_{\xi \in \bar{J}_r} p^k_{(r)(\xi)} + \sum_{i \in \bar{G}_r} (S^k_{(i)} + P^k_{(i)}) \right.$$

$$\left. \min_{i\xi \in \bar{J}_{rs}} \sum_{h=k+1}^{K} p^h_{(i)(\xi)} \right\} \qquad (8.36)$$

where $C^k_{(r)(s)}$ is the completion time of $J_{(r)(s)}$ on M_k, and $\bar{G}_r$ is the set of groups not yet sequenced, and $\bar{J}_{rs}$ and $\bar{J}_r$ are the set of jobs not yet sequenced and the set of jobs not yet sequenced in group $G_{(r)}$, respectively.

The second and third terms of the above equation are the sum of the job processing times for jobs not yet sequenced in the current group $G_{(r)}$ and the sum of the group processing times for groups not yet specified in the node, respectively. The last one represents the minimum of the sums of job processing times in the remaining stages for each of the jobs not yet sequenced.

2. Job-based bound: The job-based bound at N_{rs} is given by:

$$L_2(N_{rs}) = \max_{1 \leq k \leq K} \left[C^k_{(r)(s)} + \max_{i\xi \in \bar{J}_{rs}} \left\{ \sum_{h=k}^{K} p^h_{(i)(\xi)} \right.\right.$$

$$\left.\left. + \sum_{j\eta \in \bar{J}_{rs} \atop {j \neq i \atop \eta \neq \xi}} \min (p^k_{(j)(\eta)}, p^K_{(j)(\eta)}) + \sum_{j \in \bar{G}_r} \min(S^k_{(j)}, S^K_{(j)}) \right\} \right]$$

$$(8.37)$$

This bound expresses the fact that the total elapsed time may be determined by the total processing time for a job rather than the total processing time on a machine.

3. Composite lower bound: The composite lower bound, which is a combination of the above two bounds, is shown:

$$L_3(N_{rs}) = \max\{L_1(N_{rs}), L_2'(N_{rs})\} \qquad (8.38)$$

where $L_2'(N_{rs})$ is obtained by eliminating the bound on M_K in equation 8.37.

The branch-and-bound algorithm for determining the optimal group schedule under the criterion of the minimum makespan is as follows:

Optimizing algorithm based on the branch-and-bound method.

Step 1. Let the group level $r = 0$ and the least feasible value $L^* = \infty$. Go to step 2.

Step 2. Branch the group node N_r into $(N - r)$ group nodes N_{r+1} by placing each of the groups not yet allocated next in the sequence already determined. Set $r = r + 1$, then go to step 3.

Step 3. For each of the group nodes N_r, create job nodes N_{rs} of the job level $s = 1$ by placing each of the jobs in the group next in the sequence already determined. Go to step 4.

Step 4. Calculate the lower bound $LB(N_{rs})$ for each of the new job nodes N_{rs} by using equation 8.36, or 8.37, or 8.38.

Step 5. Find the job node having min $LB(N_{rs})$ from among the job nodes derived in step 3 or 8 in the case of $L^* = \infty$, or from among all job nodes being active in the case of $L^* \neq \infty$. (In the case of a tie, select the node with the largest value of, first, r, and then, s.) Let $LB^*(N_{rs}) = LB(N_{rs})$.) Go to step 6.

Step 6. If $LB^*(N_{rs}) < L^*$, then go to step 7. Otherwise, stop. (The group and job sequences of the node having L^* are optimal.)

Step 7. If $s < n_{(r)}$, go to step 8. Otherwise, go to step 9.

Step 8. Branch the job node N_{rs} into $(n_{(r)} - s)$ nodes N_{rs+1} by placing each of the jobs not yet allocated in group $G_{(r)}$ next in the sequence determined. Set $s = s + 1$, then go back to step 4.

Step 9. If $r < N$, then go back to step 2. Otherwise, $L^* = LN^*(N_{rs})$, and go back to step 5.

Example 8.9. Consider an eight-job, three-group, three-stage flow-shop group scheduling problem of minimizing the makespan, as shown in table 8.10. The optimal group schedule which minimizes the makespan is determined by the branch-and-bound algorithm described above. Figure 8.11

Table 8.10. Basic data for an eight-job, three-group, three-stage group scheduling problem of minimizing the makespan

Group	G_1			G_2				G_3			
Job		J_{11}	J_{12}		J_{21}	J_{22}	J_{23}		J_{31}	J_{32}	J_{33}
Setup/Processing Time	S_1^k	p_{11}^k	p_{12}^k	S_2^k	p_{21}^k	p_{22}^k	p_{23}^k	S_3^k	p_{31}^k	p_{32}^k	p_{33}^k
Stage 1	5	5	7	3	2	4	3	7	2	1	9
Stage 2	5	5	1	6	3	2	8	3	2	8	2
Stage 3	4	3	8	4	1	6	5	1	7	4	5

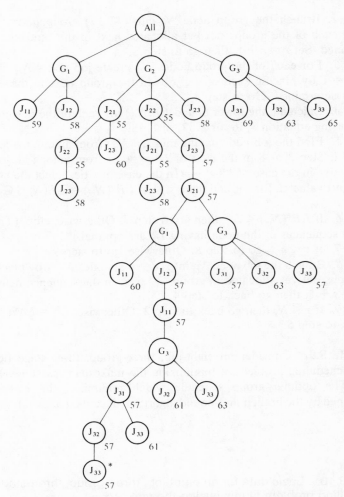

Figure 8.11.　Branching tree for Example 8.8

shows the branching tree in the case where the machine-based bound is used in the algorithm. The figures just below the job nodes indicate the lower bounds on the makespan for those nodes. For example, the detail procedure for calculating the lower bound for node $[J_{21}]$ is as follows.

According to equation 8.36, first, calculating $C_{(1)(1)}^k (k = 1, 2, 3)$,

$$C_{(1)(1)}^1 = S_{(1)}^1 + p_{(1)(1)}^1$$

$$= S_2^1 + p_{21}^1$$

$$= 3 + 2$$

$$= 5$$

$$C_{(1)(1)}^2 = \max(C_{(1)(1)}^1, S_{(1)}^2) + p_{(1)(1)}^2$$

$$= \max(C_{(1)(1)}^1, S_2^2) + p_{21}^2$$

$$= \max(5, 6) + 3$$

$$= 9$$

$$C_{(1)(1)}^3 = \max(C_{(1)(1)}^2, S_{(1)}^3) + p_{(1)(1)}^3$$

$$= \max(9, 4) + 1$$

$$= 10$$

Calculating $\Sigma_{j\in\bar{J}} p_{(1)(j)}^k$ $(k = 1, 2, 3)$, since in this case, $\bar{J}_r$ consists of J_{22} and J_{23},

$$\sum_{j\in\bar{J}_1} p_{(1)(j)}^1 = p_{(1)(2)}^1 + p_{(1)(3)}^1$$

$$= p_{22}^1 + p_{23}^1$$

$$= 4 + 3$$

$$= 7$$

$$\sum_{j\in\bar{J}_1} p_{(1)(j)}^2 = 2 + 8$$

$$= 10$$

$$\sum_{j\in\bar{J}_1} p_{(1)(j)}^3 = 6 + 5$$

$$= 11$$

Calculating $\Sigma_{i\in\bar{G}_r} (S_{(i)}^k + P_{(i)}^k)$ $(k = 1, 2, 3)$, since in this situation, $\bar{G}_r$ consists of G_1 and G_3,

$$\sum_{i\in\bar{G}_r} (S_{(i)}^1 + P_{(i)}^1) = (S_1^1 + P_1^1) + (S_3^1 + P_3^1)$$

$$= (S_1^1 + p_{11}^1 + p_{12}^1) + (S_3^1 + p_{31}^1 + p_{32}^1 + p_{33}^1)$$

$$= (5 + 5 + 7) + (7 + 2 + 1 + 9)$$

$$= 36$$

$$\sum_{i \in \bar{G}_r} (S^2_{(i)} + P^2_{(i)}) = (5 + 5 + 1) + (3 + 2 + 8 + 2)$$

$$= 26$$

$$\sum_{i \in \bar{G}_r} (S^3_{(i)} + P^3_{(i)}) = (4 + 3 + 8) + (1 + 7 + 4 + 5)$$

$$= 32$$

Calculating $\min_{i\xi \in \bar{J}_{rs}} \Sigma^K_{h=k+1} p^h_{(i)(\xi)}$ $(k = 1, 2)$, since at this instant, $\bar{J}_{rs}$ consists of $J_{11}, J_{12}, J_{22}, J_{23}, J_{31}, J_{32}$ and J_{33},

$$\min_{i\xi \in \bar{J}_{rs}} \sum_{h=2}^{3} p^h_{(i)(\xi)} = \min(p^2_{11} + p^3_{11}, p^2_{12} + p^3_{12}, p^2_{22} + p^3_{22},$$

$$p^2_{23} + p^3_{23}, p^2_{31} + p^3_{31}, p^2_{32} + p^3_{32}, p^2_{33} + p^3_{33})$$

$$= \min(5 + 3, 1 + 8, 2 + 6, 8 + 5, 2 + 7, 8 + 4, 2 + 5)$$

$$= \min(8, 9, 8, 13, 9, 12, 7)$$

$$= 7$$

$$\min_{i\xi \in \bar{J}_{rs}} \sum_{h=3}^{3} p^h_{(i)(\xi)} = \min(3, 8, 6, 5, 7, 4, 5)$$

$$= 3$$

Hence

$$LB(J_{21}) = \max(5 + 7 + 36 + 7, 9 + 10 + 26 + 3, 10 + 11 + 32)$$

$$= \max(55, 48, 53)$$

$$= 55$$

The optimal group schedule is obtained at job node with an asterisk where $r = 3$ and $s = 3$. The lower bound has the value of 57. The results show that the optimal group schedule is $G_2(J_{22} - J_{23} - J_{21}) - G_1(J_{12} - J_{11}) - G_3(J_{31} - J_{32} - J_{33})$ with the minimum makespan of 57.

8.5 Heuristic Approach to Multi-Stage Group Scheduling

The application of the branch-and-bound method to solve the group scheduling problems assures the optimal solution; it requires, however, great computational effort if the problems are large scale. Accordingly, methods of obtaining near-optimal or good solutions to these types of problems with less computational effort are required from the practical viewpoint, even though optimality is not ascertained. One such method was presented by Petrov for solving the conventional scheduling problems. Petrov's method is actually an extension of Johnson's algorithm for solving two-machine flow-shop scheduling minimizing the makespan. This method can still be extended to the multi-stage group scheduling problems.

With the use of theorems 8.8 and 8.9, heuristic procedures are developed to solve the multi-stage group scheduling problem of minimizing the makespan. One heuristic procedure using theorem 8.8 is as follows:

Heuristic procedure 1 for multi-stage group scheduling.

Step 1. Divide group setup times for G_i ($i = 1, 2, \ldots, N$) and job processing times for $J_{i\xi}$ ($i = 1, 2, \ldots, N, \xi = 1, 2, \ldots, n_i$) on K machines into two components, respectively:

$$\left. \begin{array}{l} S_i^A = \displaystyle\sum_{k=1}^{h} S_i^k \\[1em] S_i^B = \displaystyle\sum_{k=h'}^{K} S_i^k \end{array} \right\} \quad (i = 1, 2, \ldots, N) \tag{8.39}$$

$$\left. \begin{array}{l} p_{i\xi}^A = \displaystyle\sum_{k=1}^{h} p_{i\xi}^k \\[1em] p_{i\xi}^B = \displaystyle\sum_{k=h'}^{K} p_{i\xi}^k \end{array} \right\} \quad (i = 1, 2, \ldots, N, \xi = 1, 2, \ldots, n_i) \tag{8.40}$$

where $h = K/2$ and $h' = h + 1$ for even K and $h = h' = (K + 1)/2$ for odd K.

Step 2. Apply the optimizing algorithm for the two-stage flow-shop group scheduling to the groups and jobs, each of which has two fictitious group setup times given by equation 8.39 and each of which has two fictitious job processing times given by equation 8.40, respectively. The group schedule obtained is a near-optimal one.

In the above procedure, groups and jobs considered are supposed to be processed on two fictitious machines A and B. The group setup times and the job processing times for these fictitious machines are calculated by equations 8.39 and 8.40.

Another heuristic procedure which requires a less computational effort than the above procedure is developed as follows.

Job sequence for each group is determined in the same way as in the above procedure, first by calculating two fictitious job processing times for each job $J_{i\xi}$ $(i = 1, 2, \ldots, N, \xi = 1, 2, \ldots, n_i)$ with the use of equation 8.40, and then by applying Johnson's algorithm.

In order to decide group sequence, two fictitious group processing times for each group are calculated by dividing group processing times for G_i $(i = 1, 2, \ldots, N)$ on K machines into two components, as follows:

$$
\left.
\begin{array}{l}
Q_i^A = \displaystyle\sum_{k=1}^{h} Q_i^k \\[2em]
Q_i^B = \displaystyle\sum_{k=h'}^{K} Q_i^k
\end{array}
\right\} \quad (i = 1, 2, \ldots, N) \qquad (8.41)
$$

Then, group sequence is also determined by applying Johnson's algorithm to the groups, each of which has two fictitious group processing times given by equation 8.41.

The other heuristic procedure can be developed. For determining group sequence, instead of using Johnson's algorithm of the above procedure, the optimizing algorithm for the two-stage flow-shop scheduling with setup times separated is applied by using the two fictitious group setup times and total processing times of groups given by equations 8.39 and 8.40, respectively.

Example 8.10. Consider a three-group, three-stage problem, the same as shown in table 8.10.

Heuristic procedure 1. The two fictitious group setup times for G_i and the two fictitious job processing times for $J_{i\xi}$ on the two fictitious machines A and B are given in table 8.11. In this case $K = 3$, which is odd; hence, $h = h' = (3 + 1)/2 = 2$. For example, $S_1^A = 5 + 5 = 10$, $S_i^B = 5 + 4 = 9$, $p_{11}^A = 5 + 5 = 10$, $p_{11}^B = 5 + 3 = 8$.

Applying the optimizing algorithm for two-stage flow-shop group scheduling to this table, near-optimal job sequences are first determined as $J_{12} - J_{11}$, $J_{22} - J_{23} - J_{21}$, and $J_{31} - J_{32} - J_{33}$, respectively. Then the values of X_i and Y_i $(i = 1, 2, 3)$ under the job sequences determined are computed as: $[(X_1, Y_2), (X_2, Y_2), (X_3, Y_3)] = [(10, 8), (8, 12), (10, 8)]$ (for example, $X_1 = 10 - 9 + \max(8, 8 + 10 - 9) = 10$). Applying Johnson's algorithm to this list, the group sequence is decided as $G_2 - G_1 - G_3$.

Consequently, a near optimal group schedule is $G_2(J_{22} - J_{23} - J_{21}) - G_1(J_{12} - J_{11}) - G_3(J_{31} - J_{32} - J_{33})$ with the makespan of 57.

Table 8.11. Fictitious group setup times and fictitious job processing times on fictitious machines A and B

Group	G_1			G_2				G_3			
Job	J_{11}	J_{12}		J_{21}	J_{22}	J_{23}		J_{31}	J_{32}	J_{33}	
Group Setup Time/ Job Processing Time	S_1^k	p_{11}^k	p_{12}^k	S_2^k	p_{21}^k	p_{22}^k	p_{23}^k	S_3^k	p_{31}^k	p_{32}^k	p_{33}^k
Machine A	10	10	8	9	5	6	11	10	4	9	11
Machine B	9	8	9	10	4	8	13	4	9	12	7

Heuristic procedure 2. In this procedure, near-optimal job sequences are determined in the same way as in heuristic procedure 1. They are $J_{12} - J_{11}$, $J_{22} - J_{23} - J_{21}$, and $J_{31} - J_{32} - J_{33}$.

For determining group sequence, the values of Q_i^A and Q_i^B ($i = 1, 2, 3$) are computed by using equation 8.41, as $[(Q_1^A, Q_1^B), (Q_2^A, Q_2^B), Q_3^A, Q_3^B)] = [(28, 26), (31, 35), (34, 32)]$. Applying Johnson's algorithm to this list, a near-optimal group sequence is obtained as $G_2 - G_3 - G_1$. Consequently, a near-optimal group schedule is decided as $G_2(J_{22} - J_{23} - J_{21}) - G_3(J_{31} - J_{32} - J_{33}) - G_1(J_{12} - J_{11})$ with the makespan of 58.

The optimal group schedule which is determined by the branch-and-bound algorithm in the previous section is $G_2(J_{22} - J_{23} - J_{21}) - G_1(J_{12} - J_{11}) - G_3(J_{31} - J_{32} - J_{33})$ with the makespan of 57. Comparing the three group schedules obtained, one of the two schedules given by the heuristic procedures is just the same as the optimal one, while the other is somewhat different. However, the difference in the makespan value of the two schedules is not large. The branch-and-bound algorithm certainly ascertains the optimal solution, but it takes much more computation time than the heuristic procedures. Generally, the larger the problem, the larger the deviation of the solution by the heuristic procedures from the optimal solution. The most significant advantage of the heuristic procedures developed is that the computational efforts are very small to obtain a good solution, even though complete optimality may not be ascertained.

References

1. Johnson, S.M. "Optimal Two- and Three-Stage Production Schedules with Setup Times Included." *Naval Research Logistic Quarterly*, 1(1), pp. 61–68, 1954.

2. Mitten, L.G. "Sequencing *n* Jobs on Two Machines with Arbitrary Time Lags." *Management Science*, 5(3), pp. 293–298, 1959.
3. Yoshida, T., and Hitomi, K. "Optimal Two-Stage Production Scheduling with Setup Times Separated." *AIIE Transactions*, 11(3), pp. 261–263, 1979.
4. Nabeshima, I. "Some Extensions of the *m*-Machine Scheduling Problem." *Journal of the Operations Research Society of Japan*, 10(1 and 2), pp. 1–17, 1967.
5. Gupta, J.N.D. "Optimal Schedules for Special Structure Flowshops." *Naval Research Logistic Quarterly*, 22(2), pp. 255–269, 1975.
6. Szwarc, W. "Special Cases of the Flow-shop Problem." *Naval Research Logistic Quarterly*, 24(3), pp. 483–492, 1977.
7. Little, J.D.C., Murty, K.G., Sweeny, D.W., and Karel, C. "An Algorithm for the Traveling Salesman Problem." *Operations Research*, 11(6), pp. 972–989, 1963.
8. Ignall, E., and Schrage, L.E. "Application of the Branch-and-Bound Technique to Some Flow-Shop Scheduling Problems." *Operations Research*, 13(3), pp. 401–412, 1965.
9. Lomnicki, Z. "A Branch-and-Bound Algorithm for the Exact Solution of Three-Machine Scheduling Problem." *Operational Research Quarterly*, 16(1), pp. 89–101, 1965.
10. Petrov, V.A. *Flowline Group Production Planning*, translated by E. Harris. Yorkshire; National Lending Co., Chapter 7, 1966.
11. Baker, K.R. *Introduction to Sequencing and Scheduling*. New York: Wiley, 1974.
12. Yoshida, T., and Hitomi, K. "Multi-stage Production Scheduling with Setup-Time Consideration." (Japanese), *Transactions of the Japan Society of Mechanical Engineers*, 45(395), 1979.
13. Yoshida, T. "A Study of Production Scheduling (Theory of Multi-stage Group Scheduling to Minimize Total Elapsed Time)." (Japanese), *Journal of Kobe University of Commerce*, 30(5 and 6), pp. 57–76, 1979.
14. Nakamura, N., and Hitomi, K. "Analysis of Production Scheduling (Optimization of Group Scheduling on Multiple Production Systems)." (Japanese), *Transactions of the Japan Society of Mechanical Engineers*, 22(361), pp. 2964–2975, 1976.
15. Hitomi, K., and Ham, I. "Operation Scheduling for Group Technology Application." *CIRP Annals*, 25 (August 1976), pp. 419–422.

9 LAYOUT PLANNING FOR GROUP TECHNOLOGY

9.1 Essentials of Layout Planning

Together with the production planning, process planning, production scheduling, and others, an important planning activity in manufacturing firms is to determine a spatial location for a collection of physical production facilities. This is so-called layout planning. The optimal decision about this layout planning leads to the reduction of material handling times and costs, decrease of in-process inventories, the improvement of environmental conditions of workers, shortening of production lead time, increase of machine utilization, and others, thereby resulting in decrease of the total production cost.

In general, layout planning covers the following problems of different levels:

1. Plant location, that is, the selection of the site for constructing a new plant.
2. Allocation of the buildings to be constructed in the site selected.
3. Allocation of production departments, such as forging, machining, assembly, et cetera, to production areas in each building.

4. Allocation of production facilities to working areas in each department; for example, positioning of each machine tool in a machining department.

   In this chapter, discussion is mainly focused on the last two problems, especially layout planning of machine tools.

9.2 Layout Types and P-Q Analysis

In general, there are three basic types of plant layout: (1) product (or flow-line, or production-line) layout; (2) process (or functional) layout; and (3) group (-technology) (or cellular) layout. The type of layout suitable for an individual plant is dependent on the relationship between the number of product items, P, to be produced and their production quantities, Q. Generally speaking, with this P-Q analysis, a suitable pattern of plant layout is determined, as shown in figure 9.1 [1].

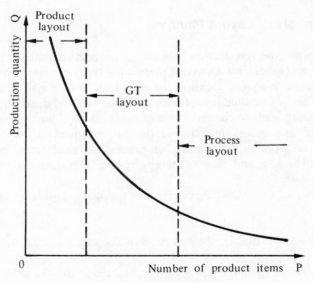

Figure 9.1.   P-Q Chart [2]

Product Layout

In case of a large ratio of Q/P, a continuous mass production is justified, and production facilities and auxiliary service equipment are located according to the process route for producing the products. An example of this layout is shown in figure 9.2.

Process Layout

In case of a small ratio of Q/P, or jobbing or small-lot production, machines, and service equipment of like types are located together as work centers in one area of the plant. An example of this layout is shown in figure 9.3.

Group Layout

In case of a medium-sized ratio of Q/P where a great variety of products can be grouped into several group cells, these grouped items are produced as apparent lots, and machines and service equipment are arranged to meet this type production. This is a pattern of layout between the previously mentioned two patterns. Group layout can be classified into three types of layout as follows through the degree of similarity of the parts in respect to manufacturing [3]:

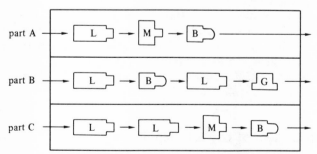

(Note) L: Lathe; M: Milling machine; G: Grinding machine; B: Boring machine.

Figure 9.2.   Product Layout [2]

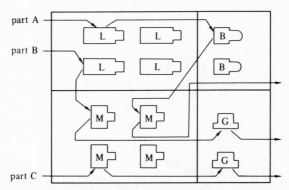

(Note) L: Lathe; M: Milling machine; G: Grinding machine; B: Boring machine.

Figure 9.3.   Product Layout [2]

1. GT *flow line*. This type of layout can be made when each of the part families to be produced has almost the same processing route resulting in the same production flow through machine tools. The GT flow-line is the highest degree of rationalization for GT layout and can take considerable advantage of mass production as in the case of product layout.

2. GT *cell*. This is a GT layout in which the production flow for each part in one or more families is not identical; therefore, a GT flow-line is not established. It is one in which all the machining operations for one or more families can be accomplished in a collection of machine tools, namely, a GT cell. Thus this cell-type layout allows feasible operation sequences depending on the types of parts.

3. GT *center*. A GT center consists of a work place laid out in such a way that a part family can be processed by the same type of operation. This type of layout is the lowest level of GT layout and very close to the functional layout. Examples of three kinds of GT layout are shown in figure 9.4.

9.3 Basic Models of Layout Planning

As mentioned previously, layout planning is a decision of spatial location of production facilities. A basic model of layout planning has been constructed as an assignment problem. A simple model of layout planning is defined next.

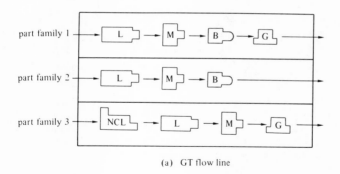

(a) GT flow line

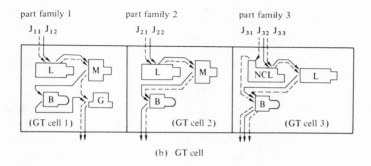

(b) GT cell

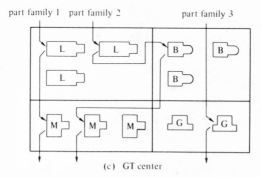

(c) GT center

(Note) L: Lathe; M: Milling machine; G: Grinding machine; B: Boring machine; NCL: NC Lathe.

Figure 9.4.   GT Layout [2]

Suppose that n new facilities are to be located, one at each site, and there are exactly n sites available for location. Let c_{ij} denote the cost of locating facility i at site j. 0-1 type variables are introduced, such that $x_{ij} = 1$ when facility i is located at site j, and $x_{ij} = 0$ otherwise. Then a simple layout planning model is formulated as the assignment problem as follows:

Minimize

$$z = \sum_{i=1}^{n} \sum_{j=1}^{n} c_{ij} x_{ij} \tag{9.1}$$

subject to

$$\left. \begin{array}{c} \sum_{j=1}^{n} x_{ij} = 1 \quad (i = 1, 2, \ldots, n) \\ \sum_{i=1}^{n} x_{ij} = 1 \quad (j = 1, 2, \ldots, n) \\ x_{ij} = 0 \text{ or } 1 \end{array} \right\} \tag{9.2}$$

This problem has exactly the same form as the one for the machine loading problem introduced in section 5.2. Hence, this problem can also be easily solved by the Hungarian method.

The above model of layout planning is a simple model and does not consider the processing flow of materials through facilities to be located. The flow of materials is usually given by the form of from-to charts showing the number of materials passing through any pair of facilities. A more practical formulation which considers the flow of materials is made next.

Let $a(i)$ denote the number of the site to which facility i is assigned and let A be the assignment vector given by $A = (a(1), a(2), \ldots, a(n))$. If six facilities are assigned to six sites according to the assignment vector $A = (2, 5, 1, 6, 4, 3)$, then facility 1 is assigned to site 2, facility 2 to site 5 and so on. Furthermore, let f_{ij} and d_{kl} denote the number of materials passing through facilities i and j and the distance between sites k and l, respectively. A measure of performance to be minimized for optimal layout planning, assigning n facilities to n sites, is given as follows:

$$C = \sum_{i=1}^{n} \sum_{j=1}^{n} f_{ij} d_{a(i)a(j)} \tag{9.3}$$

where f_{ii}'s and d_{kk}'s are zero.

This problem is referred to as a type of quadratic assignment problem and is hard to solve. Solution algorithmns based on the branch and bound method have been developed for solving this problem [4]; however, they are of no significant practical value.

9.4 Layout Planning Model for Group Technology

In general, GT layout planning includes three kinds of problems to be solved: (1) machine group (GT cell) formation; (2) the layout problem of machine groups determined; and (3) the layout problem of individual machines for each machine group. A mathematical layout model that covers all three layout problems for group technology has not yet been developed. Among the three problems of GT layout planning, the problem of formating machine groups is considered most important by many researchers.

Basically, the problem of machine grouping is defined as follows: Given the machine-part matrix showing which machines are required to produce each part, find groups of machines and families of parts in such a way that each part in a family can be fully processed in a group of machines (that is, a GT cell). A most primitive method to solve this problem is to rearrange rows and columns of the matrix on trial and error until a good solution is obtained. This method was employed in group analysis of production flow analysis by Burbidge [5]. This method is useful for problems of a relatively small number of machines and parts involved. However, it contains two difficulties: (1) this method is based on heuristics; and (2) some computational effort will be required to determine appropriate machine groups and part families for large problems.

To cope with the difficulties involved in the method, several useful methods have been developed [6–9]. Among these, the notable ones are the methods based on cluster analysis developed in the field of numerical taxonomy. Two basic methods by clustering are explained in this section.

9.4.1 Clustering Method

The clustering method developed by McAuley [6] consists of two essential steps:

1. Define a similarity coefficient showing the interdependence for each machine-part combination.
2. Cluster machines, based on similarity coefficients.

In this method, a similarity coefficient is first calculated for each pair of machines. This similarity coefficient is an indicator that describes how alike the two machines are in terms of the number of parts visiting both machines and the number of parts visiting each machine. Supposing that N_{ij} and M_{ij} are the number of parts that visit both machines i and j and the number of parts that visit one machine but not the other, respectively, the similarity coefficient for machines i and j is defined as:

$$S_{ij} = \frac{N_{ij}}{N_{ij} + M_{ij}} \qquad (9.4)$$

For example, for a machine-part matrix given by table 9.1, the similarity coefficients for all pairs of machines are calculated as follows:

$$S_{12} = \frac{2}{2 + 2} = 0.5$$

$$S_{13} = \frac{2}{2 + 3} = 0.4$$

$$S_{23} = \frac{3}{3 + 1} = 0.75$$

In the case of N machines, the total number of similarity coefficients to be calculated is $N(N-1)/2$; for the above example, $N(N-1)/2 = 3(3-1)/2 = 3$.

After calculating similarity coefficients for each pair of machines, the next problem is to determine machine groups (GT cells) by using these coefficients. In grouping machines in GT cells, a method called "cluster analysis" is employed. Cluster analysis is a technique used to form groups or similar items. Generally this method does not give any optimality in grouping of items but provides a good solution to classification problems. It clusters those items (machines) highly related with a highly specified similarity coefficient.

This clustering is successively made by lowering a specified similarity level (admission level). Hence, for each of the admission levels, clusters (GT

Table 9.1. Machine-part matrix

Machine \ Part	1	2	3	4	5
1	0	1	1	1	0
2	0	1	1	0	1
3	1	1	1	0	1

Note: "1" signifies that the part visits a machine and "0" signifies that it does not.

cell candidates) are made. The problem is how to define the similarity between two clusters (machine groups). There are several ways of estimating it. The way employed by McAuley is called "single linkage cluster analysis." This defines the similarity of the two groups as the similarity of a pair of members (one in each group) having the highest similarity between all pairs of members.

Now that clusters are represented according to the admission level, the next step is to find good clusters. For this purpose, a criterion is introduced for finding a solution that minimizes the sum of the cost of intergroup journeys and the cost of intragroup journeys. Thus a good solution is given by calculating the total journey cost for each of the possible solutions and selecting the most minimal one.

There are still two problems to be solved. One is how to calculate the distances moved by parts both between machines and between machine groups; this gives the basis of computing the journey cost. It is not calculated exactly unless both decisions as to the layout of machine groups and the layout of machines in each machine group are made. This is also dependent on the sequences of parts through machines and machine groups. Three possible layouts are assumed for machines of each machine group: (1) a straight line; (2) a rectangle; and (3) a square. The expected distance a part travels between two machines in a group of N machines is (a) $(N + 1)/3$ for a straight line, (b) $(M + L)/3$ for a rectangle in case of M rows of L machines, and (c) $2\sqrt{N}/3$ for a square. Thus the total distance for intragroup journeys for parts is computed based on this expected distance (see example 9.1).

The other problem to be solved is how to decide the ratio of intragroup journey cost to intergroup journey cost. McAuley mentioned in his paper that it does not matter since that ratio did not have any effect on the solution— even if the cost of an intergroup journey varies from four to eight times that of one unit of distance covered in an intragroup journey.

Example 9.1. Consider a simple problem as outlined in the machine-part matrix in table 9.2. The first thing to do is to calculate similarity coefficients for each pair of 10 machines. In this example, the number of similarity coefficients to be calculated is 45 ($= 10(10 - 1)/2$). Then cluster analysis is done by single linkage. The result of cluster analysis is ordinarily represented by a tree diagram called a "dendrogram" as shown in figure 9.5. The ordinate of this figure indicates a certain similarity coefficient scale from zero to one. The abscissa of the dendrogram represents the machine labels (the order of the machines is not important). The dendrogram is simply a pictorial representation of bonds of similarity between machines. Points of junction between stems along a scale in the ordinate signify that the resemblance

Table 9.2.   Machine-part matrix for example 9.1

Part \ Machine	1	2	3	4	5	6	7	8
1	1	1				1		1
2	1					1		
3		1		1				1
4	1	1				1		
5				1		1		
6		1		1				1
7				1				1
8	1	1				1		
9				1		1		
10		1				1		

between the two stems is a similarity coefficient level shown on the ordinate. Thus a set of machine groups (GT cell candidates) is easily obtained by drawing lines across the dendrogram from one to the zero level in the ordinate. For instance, at the 0.6 level of resemblance, we obtain the following four groups of machines:

1.   Machines 1, 2, 4, and 8
2.   Machines 3, 6, and 7
3.   Machines 5 and 9
4.   Machine 10.

After all, seven possible solutions are obtained from figure 9.5 as shown in table 9.3. Thus a good solution is determined by calculating the total cost of intergroup journeys and intragroup journeys for each of the solutions obtained and by selecting the one with the least cost.

The first step for determining one solution is to count the number of intergroup journeys for each solution. The next step is to calculate the total distance of intragroup journeys. Among three possible layouts for each machine group (GT cell), a straight line is to be assumed. The travel distance for each group of machines is calculated by multiplying the expected distance a part moves by the number of journeys passing through pairs of machines in that group. For example, calculate this distance for solution number 4 which has four GT cell candidates. The number of journeys passing through two machines for a GT cell candidate (machines 1, 2, 4, and 8) is 8 (3 for part 1;

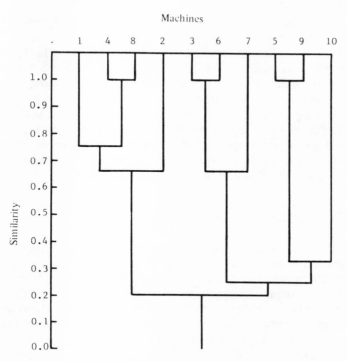

Figure 9.5.   Dendrogram

Table 9.3.   GT cell candidates

Solution Number	Number of Groups	GT Cell Candidates
1	10	Each machine in a group
2	7	(1), (2), (3,6), (4,8), (5,9), (7), (10)
3	6	(1,4,8), (2), (3,6), (5,9), (7), (10)
4	4	(1,2,4,8), (3,6,7), (5,9), (10)
5	3	(1,2,4,8), (3,6,7), (5,9,10)
6	2	(1,2,4,8), (3,5,6,7,9,10)
7	1	All machines in one group

2 for part 3; 3 for part 6; and 0 for part 8). In the same way, the numbers of intragroup journeys for three other cell candidates are obtained as 5, 2, and 0, respectively. Hence, the total distance of intragroup journeys for solution number 4 is calculated as $(4 + 1)/3 \times 8 + (3 + 1)/3 \times 5 + (2 + 1)/3 \times 2 = 22$. The number of intergroup journeys and the total distance of intragroup journeys for each solution are shown in table 9.4. By assuming that an intergroup journey cost is five times as much as one unit of distance covered by an intragroup journey, the total cost of intergroup journeys and intragroup journeys for each solution is calculated as shown in table 9.5. Thus a solution is easily determined from this table as solution number 5 with the least total cost of 34 and three GT cell candidates.

9.4.2 Rank Order Algorithm

Rank order cluster algorithm developed by King is a simple, effective analytical technique for the formation of machine-part groupings. Without calculating similarity coefficients, this algorithm can make the formation of machine-part grouping by generating diagonalized groupings of the machine-part matrix. The algorithm starts with reading the rows and columns in the matrix as binary numbers and calculates the decimal equivalent of the binary form. Then the algorithm makes use of the feature that every row or column pattern of blank or unity cell entries of the matrix can be considered as equivalent to a binary word with a corresponding unique decimal number equivalent form. Based on the equivalence, the rank order cluster algorithm for generating a solution to the machine-part grouping problem is developed as follows:

Table 9.4. Number of intergroup journeys and total distance of intragroup journeys

Solution Number	Number of Intergroup Journeys	Total Distance of Intragroup Journeys
1	18	0
2	10	8
3	7	13
4	3	22
5	2	24
6	1	34.3
7	0	66

Table 9.5. Total journey cost

Solution Number	Number of Groups	Total Cost of Intergroup Journeys and Intragroup Journeys
1	10	$(5 \times 18) + (1 \times 0) = 90$
2	7	$(5 \times 10) + (1 \times 8) = 58$
3	6	$(5 \times 7) + (1 \times 13) = 48$
4	4	$(5 \times 3) + (1 \times 22) = 37$
5	3	$(5 \times 2) + (1 \times 24) = 34*$
6	2	$(5 \times 1) + (1 \times 34.3) = 39.3$
7	1	$(5 \times 0) + (1 \times 66) = 66$

Step 1. For each row of the machine-part matrix, read the pattern of cell entries as a binary word. Rank the rows in the order of decreasing binary value. For rows with the same value, ranking is made such that the order of the rows is kept.

Step 2. If the current matrix row order is the same as the rank order just determined, then stop. Otherwise, go to step 3.

Step 3. Reform the machine-part matrix by rearranging the rows in decreasing rank order. For each column of the matrix, read the pattern of cell entries as a binary word. Rank the columns in decreasing order of binary word. For columns with the same value, ranking is made such that the order of the columns is kept.

Step 4. If the current matrix column order is the same as the rank order just determined, then stop. otherwise, go to step 5.

Step 5. Reform the machine-part matrix by rearranging the columns in decreasing rank order. Go back to step 1.

Example 9.2. Consider a machine-part grouping formation problem in which the machine-part matrix is given in table 9.2, the same table as in example 9.1. Now apply the rank order cluster algorithm to this problem. The process may be summarized as follows:

Step 1. The decimal equivalents of the binary number for rows are given at the righthand side of the matrix as shown in table 9.6. For example, the first row is, in binary word, 10100101 which has the decimal equivalent of $1 \times 2^7 + 0 \times 2^6 + 1 \times 2^5 + 0 \times 2^4 + 0 \times 2^3 + 1 \times 2^2 + 0 \times 2^1 + 1 \times 2^0 = 165$. The rank order of these decimal numbers is also given at the righthand side of the matrix.

Step 2. The rank order of rows just determined is different from the current row order.

Table 9.6.   Machine-part matrix

	Binary Weight									
	2^7	2^6	2^5	2^4	2^3	2^2	2^1	2^0		
	Part									
	1	2	3	4	5	6	7	8	Decimal	Rank
Machine									Equivalent	Order
1	1	1		1		1			165	1
2	1					1			132	4
3		1		1			1		73	5
4	1	1		1					164	2
5			1			1			18	8
6		1		1			1		73	6
7				1			1		9	10
8	1	1		1					164	3
9			1			1			18	9
10		1					1		66	7

Step 3. By rearranging the rows in order of decreasing rank, we obtain table 9.7. The decimal equivalents of the binary numbers for columns are given at the bottom of the matrix. The rank order of the columns is given just below the decimal numbers.

Step 4. The rank order of the columns just determined is also different from the current column order.

Step 5. By rearranging the columns in order of decreasing rank, we obtain table 9.8. Go back to step 1.

Steps 1, 2, and 3. The matrix as shown in table 9.9 is obtained through these steps.

Step 4. The rank order of the columns just determined is also different from the current column order.

Step 5. The machine-part matrix as shown in table 9.10 is obtained by this step.

Steps 1 and 2. The rank order of rows just determined is the same as the current row order. Stop. From the last machine-part matrix, machine-part grouping is determined as (machines 1, 2, 4, and 8 and parts 1, 3, and 6), (machines 3, 6, and 7 and parts 2, 5, and 8), and (machines 5, 9, and 10 and parts 4 and 7).

Although the data of the final matrix of this example are not divided into distinct diagonalized groups, three machine groups (i.e., (1, 2, 4, 8), (3, 6, 7),

Table 9.7. Rearranged machine-part matrix (1)

Machine \ Part	1	2	3	4	5	6	7	8	Binary Weight
1	1		1			1		1	2^9
4	1		1			1			2^8
8	1		1			1			2^7
2	1					1			2^6
3		1			1			1	2^5
6		1			1			1	2^4
10		1					1		2^3
5				1			1		2^2
9				1			1		2^1
7					1			1	2^0
Decimal Equivalent	960	56	896	6	49	960	14	560	
Rank Order	1	5	3	8	6	2	7	4	

Table 9.8. Rearranged machine-part matrix (2)

Machine \ Part	1	6	3	8	2	5	7	4	Decimal Equivalent	Rank Order
1	1	1	1	1					240	1
4	1	1	1						224	2
8	1	1	1						224	3
2	1	1							192	4
3				1	1	1			28	5
6				1	1	1			28	6
10					1		1		10	8
5							1	1	3	9
9							1	1	3	10
7				1		1			20	7

Table 9.9. Rearranged machine-part matrix (3)

Part / Machine	1	6	3	8	2	5	7	4
1	1	1	1	1				
4	1	1	1					
8	1	1	1					
2	1	1						
3				1	1	1		
6				1	1	1		
7				1		1		
10					1		1	
5							1	1
9							1	1
Decimal Equivalent	960	960	896	568	52	56	7	3
Rank Order	1	2	3	4	6	5	7	8

Table 9.10. Final machine-part matrix

Part / Machine	1	6	3	8	5	2	7	4	Decimal Equivalent	Rank Order
1	1	1	1	1					240	1
4	1	1	1						224	2
8	1	1	1						224	3
2	1	1							192	4
3				1	1	1			28	5
6				1	1	1			28	6
7				1	1				24	7
10						1	1		6	8
5							1	1	3	9
9							1	1	3	10

and (5, 9, 10)) are easily suggested as GT cell candidates. However, this is not always the case. Rank order cluster algorithm has the ability to deal with such cases. One method for overcoming the difficulty is to deal with the data, such as the two processings of part 8 on machine 1 and part 2 on machine 10 in table 9.10 as exceptional elements. That is, they are considered to be equivalent to blank entries. The other method is to provide duplicate machines for a machine (bottleneck machine) that causes the restriction on division of the matrix into mutually exclusive groups to the extent that each part operation is performed by one such machine. By making use of these methods, rank order cluster algorithm works well in the case of exceptional elements or bottleneck machines. King, who developed the rank order cluster algorithm, asserts that this is the major advantage of the algorithm over the other ones for machine-part formation problems.

References

1. Hitomi, K. *Manufacturing Systems Engineering*. London: Taylor & Francis: p. 66, 1979.
2. Hitomi, K. (ed.) *Production Management Systems by Group Technology*. (Japanese), Tokyo: Daily Technical Newspaper Co., 1981.
3. Arn, E.A. *Group Technology*. Berlin: Springer-Verlag, 1975.
4. Gilmore, P.C. "Optimal and Suboptimal Algorithm for the Quadratic Assignment Problem." *Journal of Society for Industrial and Applied Mathematics*, 10(2), pp. 324–342, 1962.
5. Burbidge, J.L. "Production Flow Analysis." *Production Engineer* (April/May 1971), pp. 139–152.
6. McAuley, J. "Machine Grouping for Efficient Production." *Production Engineer* (February 1972), pp. 53–57.
7. King, J.R. "Machine-Component Grouping in Production Flow Analysis: An Approach Using a Rank Order Clustering Algorithm." *International Journal of Production Research*, 18(2), pp. 213–232, 1980.
8. Rajagopalan, R., and Batra, J.L. "Design of Cellular Production Systems: A Graph-Theoretic Approach." *International Journal of Production Research*, 13(6), pp. 567–599, 1975.
9. Gongaware, R., and Ham, I. "Cluster Analysis Application for Group Technology Manufacturing Systems." *9th NAMRC*, pp. 503–508, 1981.

10 GROUP TECHNOLOGY AND OTHER RELATED TOPICS

10.1 GT and MRP

10.1.1 Material Requirements Planning

Material requirements planning (abbreviated MRP), known as time-phased requirements planning, is a computer-based production planning and control system that is designed to work well for discrete production [1]. Discrete products such as automobile and machine tools are made up of a number of components which often form a hierarchial structure. Hence, whether the discrete products are efficiently produced according to their production schedule or not depends highly on the establishment of an effective production and control system that guarantees that components composing the products are available in necessary quantities when needed.

The conventional reorder point control systems, mainly used for controlling inventories of independent items, is not appropriate for the components that are dependent items directly related to the demand for higher level items in the product structures. The demands of the components are not to be forecasted but are calculated based on a master production schedule (production schedule of end items). MRP calculates the demand (requirements) of the components and controls the inventories of them.

A basic function of a MRP system is shown in figure 10.1. Three major inputs into a MRP system are as follows:

1. *Master production schedule (MPS)*. This outlines which products (end items), how many are produced and when they are to be delivered to customers.
2. *Bill of materials (BOM)*. This file defines the product structure of products.
3. *Inventory status records*. This file contains various aspects of information on inventory items—item master data such as item identifications, lead times, order quantities, rule of lot sizing, and others. Also included are inventory status data such as on-hand inventory status, scheduled receipts, and others.

Based on these three inputs, MRP computes how many of each component in all levels in the product structure are required and when they are needed by exploding the requirements of the products into successively lower levels. The computational outputs of this MRP calculation include reports on which components (including raw materials, subassembly, and assembly) should be ordered for purchasing, manufacturing, assembling, as well as when to order. This is determined by offsetting the lead time for each component.

It is necessary to check the feasibility of executing or not executing the plan of time-phased requirements. This is accomplished by converting the requirements into their production capacity requirements by time period assigned; it is capacity requirements planning (CRP) that performs this task. If the difference between the capacity requirements resulting from this conversion and the available capacity is not too large, adjustment is made by utilizing overtime, extra shifts, subcontracting, and others. If sufficient production capacity is not available by the above adjustment, the master production schedule must be revised or the existing capacity of the work forces and production facilities must be expanded. It is worth noting that the MRP calculation assumes that the master production schedule is feasible and an adequate capacity exists to meet its requirements.

10.1.2 Integration of GT and MRP

As mentioned throughout this book, group technology is one of the useful approaches to multi-product, small lot-sized production. On the other hand,

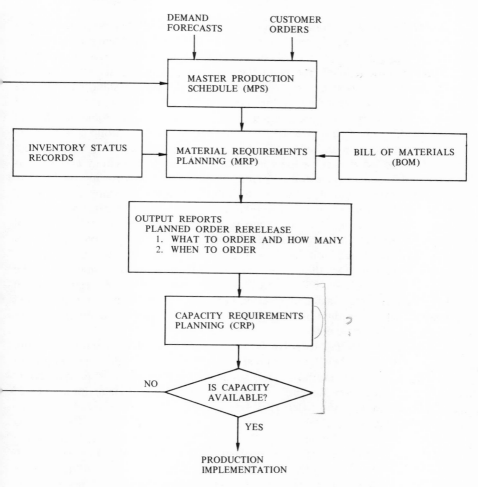

Figure 10.1. Structure of MRP system

MRP is an effective production and control system for discrete production in which various components for the required products are often produced in small or medium lot sizes. Hence, both group technology and MRP seem to be effective approaches to multi-product, small- or medium-lot-sized production or discrete production. Unfortunately, each of these techniques has several drawbacks in practice. Hence, we try to effectively combine group technology and MRP to establish a more proper production and control system for multi-product, small- or medium-lot-sized production or discrete production. In most cases, products made in discrete production are made up of a large number of components that form a hierarchical structure. Among various components in the products, there usually exists a large number of components (or parts) that may fall into the same part families classified by the group technology concept. These similar components judged from the standpoint of the group technology concept can be found in different levels of product structures that lead to the possibility of group processing in the machine shop and even group assembling in the assembly shop.

The second reason for the compatibility of group technology and MRP is the difference in operations—management fields that two approaches can cover. Group technology is a philosophy or concept in which similar parts are identified and combined to take advantage of their similarity in design and manufacturing. Hence, group technology can provide only a way of making production more efficient by utilizing the similarity of parts and is not directly concerned with the very practical and important time-phase aspects of production. On the other hand, MRP is a system that gives the requirements of the components and the exact times of need for them according to the master production schedule. As such, it is not concerned with how the orders for producing or purchasing the components are accomplished efficiently.

The next problem to solve is whether it is possible to integrate group technology and MRP to establish an effective production planning and control system for multi-product, small- or medium-lot-sized production or discrete production. Recently, some research has been done on integration of group technology and MRP [2,3,4,5].

Some researchers have proposed the use of single-cycle, single-phase ordering (period batch control) as an ordering policy for promoting production efficiency of group production in GT cells [6]. In period batch control, all parts are ordered for purchasing, manufacturing, and assembling in the same cycle. The ordering is issued based on "explosion" from a series of period production plans, and exact quantities of parts required to meet the production plan in each period are ordered. Employment of this technique as an ordering policy will give a production system much flexibility and take advantage of setup time reduction; this is a most significant advantage of group technology applications.

Since the shorter throughput time and lead time attained by group technology applications make it possible to work with much shorter periods of planning time, the period batch control ordering policy will work much more efficiently with group technology. This ordering policy matches well with the requirements of MRP, which employs a short time period such as a week or ten days as the time unit of planning. In addition, several advantages such as a shorter and predictable lead time, reduction of material handling, simplification of material flow, easiness of control in shop floor (GT cells), and others (all attained through group technology applications) make a MRP system function well in practice.

Thus integration of group technology and MRP seems to establish an effective production planning and control system. However, some research dealing with this integration gives only a framework for a GT-based MRP system. The remaining problem to be solved is how to establish a practical, executable GT-based MRP system. The following section describes such an attempt to integrate group technology and MRP.

10.1.3 Group Scheduling and MRP

Neither the schedule necessary within each specified time period to which parts are assigned for production nor the advantage of implementing the use of part family classification are limitations of MRP. On the other hand, group scheduling (dealt with in chapters 7 and 8) does not consider time-phase aspects of production. That is, a typical group scheduling assumes that all parts under consideration are available at the beginning of the time period. To cope with these limitations, an integrated system is constructed by suitably combining group scheduling and MRP. Such a system is one of the answers to the various questions faced when there is separate introduction of group technology and MRP in a production system.

A procedure for integrated applications of group scheduling and MRP may be broken down into a series of steps as listed below [5]:

Step 1. Gather the data normally required for both the group technology and MRP concepts (that is, parts and their description, machine capabilities, a breakdown of each final product into its individual components, a forecast of final product demand, et cetera).

Step 2. Use group technology to determine part families. Designate each family as G_i ($i = 1, 2, \ldots, N$).

Step 3. Use MRP to assign each component part to a specific time period.

Step 4. Arrange the component part/time period assignments of step 3 according to the part family groups of step 2.

Step 5. Use a suitable group scheduling algorithm to determine the optimal schedule for all those parts within a given group for each time period.

A simplified illustration to explain the procedure is given in tables 10.1, 10.2, and 10.3. Let us assume that five parts are to be produced within a jobshop. These parts, designated as A, B, C, D, and E, respectively, are used to form certain final products, it would be impractical to further subdivide them. Using group technology, we are able to divide the five parts into two part families, designated simply as G_1 and G_2.

The number of units required for each part for a certain month have been determined to be: A = 60, B = 60, C = 60, D = 30, and E = 50. This information has been summarized in table 10.1. However, if a group scheduling algorithm is used alone on the data given in table 10.1, such a schedule could well violate specific due date constraints. For example, one might schedule 60 units of part A for production in week 4, whereas 15 of these are actually needed in week 1.

Using MRP, the precise number of each part on a short-term (e.g., weekly) basis, may be determined. Table 10.2 illustrates such an MRP output for this example. This table gives the number of units of each part needed in each week of the month under consideration but does nothing to answer the question as to what is the optimal schedule within each week.

Thus to take full advantage of the integrated group technology/MRP system, tables 10.1 and 10.2 are combined into the integrated form of table 10.3. Next, by applying an appropriate scheduling algorithm to those sets of parts within a common group and week, we may obtain an optimal schedule for each week of the entire month that takes advantage of the group technology-induced flow shop as well as the MRP-derived due date considerations.

Table 10.1. Part-family example

Group	Part Code Number	Part Name	Units Required during Month
G_1	6212–023	A	60
	6212–015	B	60
	6212–083	D	30
G_2	5333–125	C	60
	5333–186	E	50

Table 10.2.   Weekly part assignments by MRP

Part Code Number	Part Name	Planned Order Release Week 1	2	3	4
6212–023	A	30	30	0	0
6212–015	B	15	15	15	15
5333–125	C	20	20	10	10
6212–083	D	10	10	5	5
5333–186	E	15	15	10	10

10.2 GT and CAD/CAM

10.2.1 Basic Approach

Development and implementation of computer-aided design (CAD) and computer-aided manufacturing (CAM) in the manufacturing industry lead to more integrated applications of group technology concept. It has been recognized that group technology is an essential element of the foundation for successful development and implementation of CAD/CAM through applications of the part-family concept based on geometrical and processing similarities between parts. This approach creates a compatible, economic basis for evolution of computer automation in batch manufacturing through increased use of hierarchical computer control and multi-station NC manufacturing systems.

Table 10.3.   Combined GT/MRP data

Group	Part Code Number	Part Name	Planned Order Release Week 1	2	3	4
G_1	6212–023	A	30	30	0	0
	6212–015	B	15	15	15	15
	6212–083	D	10	10	5	5
G_2	5333–125	C	20	20	10	10
	5333–186	E	15	15	10	10

A part classification system which is an integral part of, and has been used as an essential tool of, group technology applications can also be evolved as a means of describing parts in a form that can be integrated readily into a computer data base structure that links design and production. This computer data base is a key for successful development and implementation of CAD which effectively uses a computer peripheral information-processing unit to create or modify an engineering design of products. The data base plays an important role in groupings of part families, machine groups/cells, tooling setups, and so on, and also provides a data basis for computer-aided process planning. An essential role of implementation of group technology concept for an integrated approach of CAD/CAM, (i.e., computer integrated

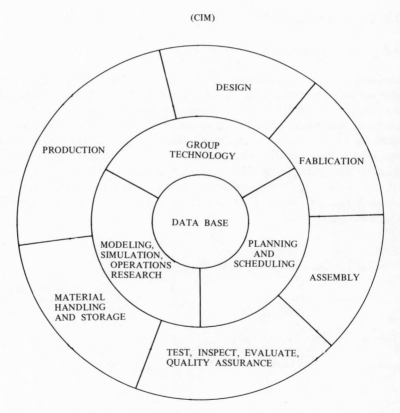

Figure 10.2. Integrated Computer Aided Manufacturing (ICAM) and Group Technology [7]

manufacturing (CIM)) has been well indicated in figure 10.2 [7]. As CIM progresses for further developments in more generative approaches for design, planning, production, group technology should evolve to accommodate these advancements in all areas of manufacturing. Therefore, for successful implementation of CIM, further development and improvement of software for group technology implementation is needed.

It is obvious that group technology will evolve as the future manufacturing systems advance with significant influence. The role of group technology will be more effective with further innovative advancements in theory and application to meet these future challenges.

10.2.2 Computer-Aided Process Planning

One of the most important aspects for successful implementation of CIM systems is computer-aided process planning. An automated process planning is an essential need for successful CIM implementation by providing a basis for logical and rational approach to the production of parts for optimum manufacturing productivity.

Computer-aided process planning is developed either by using the variant process or the generative process. Most of the current process planning systems are either a variant type or a semigenerative type. The variant technique (i.e., retrieval technique) is based on part families using a suitable classification and coding system and the given data base of standard process routes to retrieval for editing. The generative technique creates a process plan for a particular part using suitable optimum logic and data base as well. In recent years, many efforts have been made to develop a generative type process planning by various interest groups. The flow diagram of a variant type system developed by CAM-I (Computer-Aided Manufacturing-International) [8] is shown in figure 10.3.

The basic approach for developing a computer-aided process planning system is to develop a decision-making framework based on suitable algorithms or logic flow diagrams. Regardless of whether it is a variant or a generative system, group technology still plays an important role in developing a data base and providing and effective information retrieval system.

10.2.3 GT and Numerical Control

Group technology may assist in making economic justification for the use of sophisticated, expensive NC machines and/or special tooling that may have

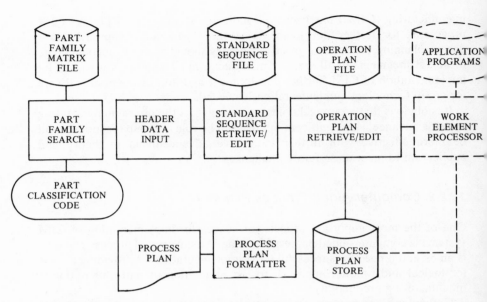

Figure 10.3. Flow diagram for computer-automated process planning by CAM-I [8]

been too costly for batch-type production. The advantages of NC-type machine tools are usually outweighed by the problems and costs of production planning and tooling, low utilization, long setup times, and so forth. With proper group technology applications, these problems can be reduced to such an extent that it becomes advantageous to use NC equipment that otherwise might be uneconomical. This is particularly true of current expensive machining-center-type NC machines.

Many advantages claimed for NC machine tools are also of great importance in a group technology environment. While NC machine tools provide the capability to produce small batches of components economically by reducing setup time, group technology offers the same through effective group scheduling. Combined utilization of special features of NC machine tools and group technology enable maximum benefits of both.

One of the important applications of group technology is a software development of NC machining called "Part-family Programming" [9]. Part-family programming is a NC program system that groups common or similar program elements for machining of part families into a master computer program. The master computer program is a permanent base from which a

NC tape can be prepared for any part in the part family. Therefore part-family programming improves the economics of NC operations by reducing programming costs, maintenance costs, and operation costs.

10.2.4 Machining Center and Multi-Station Manufacturing Systems

A NC machining center is characteristically a machine group that is capable of doing the work of several conventional machine tools by one machine. These NC machining centers have the same effect of group layout, i.e., GT layout. Therefore, machining centers may be considered as machine groups or cells, with the capability of reducing lead time and in-process inventory. Also, to improve the loading efficiency of expensive machining centers, it is desirable to utilize these machining centers under a GT environment. For selection and installation of a machining center, it is advisable to consider it as a part of the total factory system so that the maximum benefits of such a system can be obtained by more effective loading through part-family grouping and group scheduling.

With group technology applications in the layout and organization of a factory, its manpower and equipment on a part-family basis rather than a functional basis, a successful CIM program can be achieved. Evolution of CNC (computer numerical control) and DNC (direct numerical control) is also related to group technology through the computer hierarchy. As CNC type mini-computer control of the individual NC machines or machining centers in a cell is brought together, eventually it will provide a sound basis for overall DNC of the cells. By connecting all the cells or centers in the factory with a large computer, it is possible to achieve automation of the total factory systems.

One of the future trends of CIM is multi-station manufacturing systems or flexible manufacturing system (FMS), which also involves evolution of the GT cells. As the number of NC machining centers and cells under CNC/DNC systems increases, more economic operations become essential through full automation and integration of tool and work handling and transfer within the cell and between the cells using robots by effective group scheduling.

The final step in the evolution of CIM is, of course, the computer-integrated automatic factory system operating under GT environments. The overall concept for optimum operations of the automated factory system is based on the use of GT cells, each devoted to the production of given part families. Each cell may be controlled by a built-in microcomputer, and the overall computer system for the plant is hierarchical in nature. Middle-level computers control and coordinate the operation and the scheduling of one or more cells, while the overall production system is being controlled by a central main-frame computer.

10.3 GT and Engineering Economy

10.3.1 Economic Benefits and Justification

It is expected that successful implementation of group technology will certainly lead to improvements for more effective design, less stock and fewer purchases, simplified production planning and control, optimum sequencing and loading, reduced tooling and setup time, reduced work-in-process inventories, shorter production time, more efficient utilization of expensive machines, and so on, as indicated in figure 10.4.

Analysis of these economic gains through suitable cost analysis of specific applications by comparing the economic benefits of both the current conventional method and the proposed group technology method is essential.

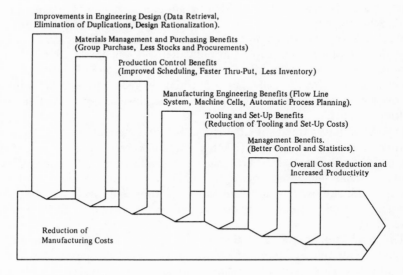

Figure 10.4. Reduction of manufacturing costs through group technology applications

Economic justification is an important step for the successful implementation of group technology. Various formulas and procedures have been proposed for such analysis, and an example of economic analysis of group tooling is presented in the next subsection.

10.3.2 Economic Analysis of Group Tooling

In production applications of group technology, part-family concept leads to the rationalization of tool designs and the reduction of tooling requirements and setups. These benefits result in reduction of tooling costs and eventually production costs as a whole. To justify the economic benefit of group tooling in comparison with the conventional tooling methods, a cost analysis [10] can be made as given below:

Conventional tooling methods. The total tooling cost, ($), of the conventional tooling methods using p different jigs or fixtures is

$$C_{tw1} = \sum_{i=1}^{p} C_{w1(i)} \qquad (10.1)$$

where C_{w1} is the cost of a jig or fixture of the conventional method, $, and p is the number of different jigs or fixtures used (also possibly number of different parts to be produced).

Group tooling method. The total cost, ($), for the group tooling using a group jig or fixture with q different adapters is

$$C_{tw2} = \sum_{i=1}^{q} C_{a(i)} + C_{w2} \qquad (10.2)$$

where C_{w2} is the cost of a group jig or fixture, ($), C_a is the cost of an adapter, and q is the number of adapters used for the production of a family of parts.

Then, unit tooling costs, ($/pc), are calculated as follows:

$$C_{u1} = \frac{C_{tw1}}{n} = \frac{1}{n} \sum_{i=1}^{p} C_{w1(i)} \qquad (10.3)$$

for the conventional tooling method; and

$$C_{u2} = \frac{C_{tw2}}{n} = \frac{1}{n} \left[\sum_{i=1}^{q} C_{a(i)} + C_{w2} \right] \qquad (10.4)$$

for the group tooling method, where n is the number of parts produced.

Table 10.4. Tooling costs for conventional and group tooling methods (in dollars)

Item	Conventional Tooling Method	Group Tooling Method
Cost of the drill jig (C_w)	800	2000
Number of jigs required (p)	6	1
Cost of an adapter (C_a)	—	500
Number of adapters required (q)	—	5

Note: Number of pieces per a part to be produced: 400

An example of the total tooling costs (C_{tw}) and the unit tooling costs (C_u) of the conventional tooling method and the group tooling method, in relation to the number of different parts in the part family or the group, are computed and listed in tables 10.4 and 10.5. The tooling cost (C_{tw}) and the unit tooling costs (C_u) as a function of the number of parts in the part family or group are plotted in figure 10.5.

As shown in these graphs, the total tooling costs for the conventional tooling method increase more than that of the group tooling method.

Table 10.5. Computed example of tooling costs for comparison in dollars

Number of Different Parts in Part Family	Conventional Method C_{tw1}	C_{u1}	Group Tooling Method C_{tw2}	C_{u2}
1	800	2.0	2,500	6.25
2	1,600	2.0	3,000	3.75
3	2,400	2.0	3,500	2.92
4	3,200	2.0	4,000	2.50
5	4,000	2.0	4,500	2.25
6	4,800	2.0	5,000	2.08
7	5,600	2.0	5,500	1.96
8	6,400	2.0	6,000	1.88
9	7,200	2.0	6,500	1.81
10	8,000	2.0	7,000	1.75
15	12,000	2.0	9,500	1.58
20	16,000	2.0	12,000	1.50

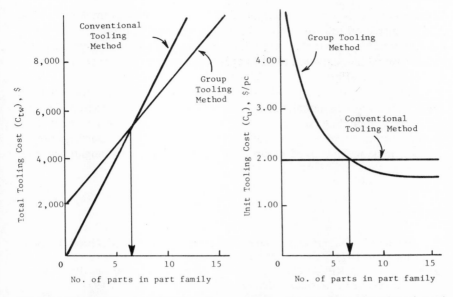

Figure 10.5. Comparative tooling cost analysis of conventional and group tooling methods (refer to tables 10.4 and 10.5)

Meanwhile, the unit tooling costs for the group tooling methods become far more economical compared to the conventional tooling method as the number of parts in the part family increase. The unit tooling cost decreases sharply up to a marginal point at which reduction of the unit tooling cost is leveled off. It should be noted that both the total tooling costs and the unit tooling costs have the break-even points.

    In comparison of the conventional and GT methods, there are many other items to be analyzed including group machining costs, group scheduling costs, group production costs, and so on. These analyses are not discussed in this book.

10.4 GT and Management Problems

It is common practice to require a high degree of cooperation between interest groups or departments in the company for implementation of a new system. Unfortunately, however, the necessary cooperation in a company is usually lacking. For successful GT implementation, it is essential to have close cooperation between all departments involved in the company.

Whenever there is any form of change of systems or way of thinking, a great deal of suspicion follows, and there might be some resistance to changes. Introduction of group technology will be no exception to this phenomenon; it requires constant education to be familiar with the new concept and accept it for cooperative effort.

Although group technology is effective and successful, the effective applications are dependent not only upon its technical characteristics, but also other, including social, factors [11]. Successful group technology applications also enhance job satisfaction through worker participation in decision making, improved group-team relationships, and heightened consciousness.

References

1. Orlichy, J. *Material Requirements Planning*. New York: McGraw-Hill Book Company, 1975.
2. New, C. "MRP & GT, A New Strategy for Component Production." *Production and Inventory Management*, 18(3), pp. 50–62, 1977.
3. Suresh, N.C. "Optimizing Intermittent Production Systems through Group Technology and an MRP System." *Production and Inventory Management*, 24(4), pp. 77–84, 1979.
4. Hyer, N.L. "MRP/GT: A Framework for Production Planning and Control of Cellular Manufacturing." *Decision Sciences*, 13, pp. 681–701, 1978.
5. Sato, N., Ignizio, J., and Ham, I. "Group Technology and Material Requirements Planning: An Integrated Methodology for Production Control." *CIRP Annals*, 28 (August 1978), pp. 471–473.
6. Burbidge, J.L. *Group Technology in the Engineering Industry*. London: Mechanical Engineering Publications, Ltd., 1979.
7. Wisnosky, D. "An Overview of the Air Force Program for Integrated Computer Aided Manufacturing." *SME Paper* #77-254, 1977.
8. CAM-I. *Seminar Proceedings*. June 1975 (#p-75-ppp-01) and January 1976 (#p-76-ppp-01), Arlington, Tx.: Computer Aided Manufacturing-International.
9. Hayner, C. "New Route to NC Productivity: Family Programming." *Metalworking Economics* (November 1969), pp. 2–10.
10. Mirofanov, S.P. *Scientific Principles of Group Technology*. (Russian text published in 1959), translated into English by E. Harris, National Lending Library for Science and Technology, U.K., 1966.
11. Burbidge, J.L. "Report on a Study of the Effects of Group Production Methods on the Humanization of Work." *ILO Report*, Turino, Italy: Center of Advanced Technology & Vocational Trading, 1974.

Index